Fears and anxieties

Fears and Anxieties

Don Rowan and Caroline Eayrs

Longman
London and New York

Longman Group UK Limited
Longman House, Burnt Mill, Harlow
Essex CM20 2JE, England
and Associated Companies throughout the world.

*Published in the United States of America
by Longman Inc., New York*

© Donald C Rowan and Caroline Eayrs

First published 1987

British Library Cataloguing in Publication Data
Rowan, Donald C.
  Fears and anxieties. —— (Longman applied
  psychology)
  1. Anxiety
  I. Title   II. Eayrs, Caroline
  616.85′223   RC531

ISBN 0-582-29624-2

Library of Congress Cataloguing in Publication Data
Rowan, Donald C., 1951–
  Fears and anxieties.
  (Longman applied psychology)
  Bibliography: p.
  Includes index.
  1. Anxiety.   2. Fear.   3. Psychiatry.   I. Eayrs,
Caroline, 1953– .   II. Title.   III. Series.
RC531.R69 1987   616.85′223   86–15276
ISBN 0-582-29624-2

Set in 9½/11pt Compedit Times
Produced by Longman Group (FE) Limited
Printed in Hong Kong

Contents

Editor's preface

In most areas of applied psychology there is no shortage of hardback textbooks many hundreds of pages in length. They give a broad coverage of the total field but rarely in sufficient detail in any one topic area for undergraduates, particularly honours students. This is even more true for trainees and professionals in such areas as clinical psychology.

The Longman Applied Psychology series consists of authoritative short books each concerned with a specific aspect of applied psychology. The brief given to the authors of this series was to describe the current state of knowledge in the area, how that knowledge is applied to the solution of practical problems and what new developments of real-life relevance may be expected in the near future. The twelve books which have been commissioned so far are concerned mainly with clinical psychology, defined very broadly. Topics range from gambling to ageing and from the chemical control of behaviour to social factors in mental illness.

The books go into sufficient depth for the needs of students at all levels and professionals yet remain well within the grasp of the interested general reader. A number of groups will find their educational and professional needs or their personal interests met by this series: professional psychologists and those in training (clinical, educational, occupational, etc.); psychology undergraduates; under-graduate students in other disciplines which include aspects of applied psychology (e.g. social administration, sociology, management, and particularly medicine); professionals and trainee professionals in fields outside psychology, but which draw on applications of psychology (doctors of all kinds, particularly psychiatrists and general practitioners, social workers, nurses, particularly psychiatric nurses, counsellors — such as school, vocational and marital — and personnel managers).

Finally, members of the general public who have been introduced to a particular topic by the increasing number of well-informed and well-presented newspaper articles and television programmes will be able to follow it up and pursue it in more depth.

Philip Feldman

Acknowledgements

We are indebted to the following for permission to reproduce copyright material:

Consulting Psychologist Press Inc. for Table from part of 'Form 1 and 2' *State Trait Anxiety Inventory* by Charles Spielburger and Assoc. Copyright 1967, 1983; Institute for Rational–Emotive Therapy for modified extracts from *The Essence of Rational Psychology: A Comprehensive Approach to Treatment* by A. Ellis, New York: Inst. for Rational-Emotive Therapy, and from *Reason and Emotion in Psychotherapy* by A. Ellis, New York: Citadel Press, 1962. Copyright by Inst. for Rational–Emotive Therapy.

Introduction

Pat is a 24-year-old married woman who enjoys life and feels that things are working out well for her. She had recently moved to a more interesting, stimulating office where she had a job as a secretary and she and her husband were putting down roots in preparation to starting a family. Everything seemed perfect except for one little problem which Pat was almost too embarrassed to admit.

She had never liked worms as a child, and was teased about her fear by her fisherman brother, but she had coped well enough and her mother had put it down to a passing childhood foible. However, over the last two years Pat's dislike of worms had developed from a niggling anxiety to a severely incapacitating fear. It had reached the point when the mere thought of going into the garden to hang out the washing had become sufficient to make her tremble and feel nauseous. If she walked down a pavement next to a grass verge she would have to move out on to the road so as to be further from the grass lest a worm appear. Once, when taken by surprise at seeing a worm crawl out of the grass she had fled across a busy road, narrowly missing the passing traffic, so severe had her fear become.

She felt slightly less worried when walking with another person. She attributed this to being preoccupied with concealing her anxiety because she was horrified that someone else may find out and ridicule her.

This fear of worms was not only making her feel wretchedly stupid and eating away at her self-confidence, it was also causing great inconvenience by her avoidance of the garden, parks, grass verges and so forth. However, in spite of repeatedly telling herself not to be so foolish and irrational Pat just could not seem to shake off the fearful thoughts. Eventually Pat confided in her husband and was considerably relieved that he took her completely seriously and accompanied her to their GP, by whom she was referred to a specialist for treatment.

The interesting point in Pat's case is the *specificity* of the fear. In spite of her enormous fear of worms she did not worry unduly about other similar creatures such as snails, snakes or slugs. The only exception to this was a strong dislike of maggots. On the other hand, take the case of *Bill* . . .

Bill is a 36-year-old engineer who, until four years ago, boasted of never having to take a day off work through illness. He was satisfied with his job, with the company he had been with since leaving university, and was doing well in the promotion stakes. All this changed one day when, while attending a meeting, he felt peculiar and collapsed, and concerned colleagues had him taken to hospital. Various tests were conducted, but no illness was discovered and he was discharged home.

Since that time he has experienced episodes of dizziness and shakiness accompanied by feelings of tightness and pains across his chest. The attacks have gradually increased in frequency and now they occur not only at work but also at home, in shops, and in the car, in fact anywhere and usually without warning. On occasions, he has had to grab people or objects in the street because he felt he would overbalance. He has become convinced that he must have a heart problem and he is preoccupied that either the doctor has missed some vital clue to his condition, or else does not want to break the bad news! He now finds it difficult to concentrate on anything for very long and lacks the confidence to go out.

His friends are very concerned that he has become

depressed and a recluse. He has become less efficient at his job, and avoids meetings or other events where he fears an attack might occur. Although his boss has so far been sympathetic and understanding, Bill is extremely worried that he will not be able to continue in his present employment for much longer. Bill places a good deal of emphasis on achievement and success in his job, and losing it would be a devastating blow.

Similar symptoms were experienced by *Lyn*, a young mother of two small children. She has experienced numbness from head to toe, palpitations, a 'swimming' head, shakiness and weakness in her arms and legs. The panic attacks which she has described have been so severe that she now hardly dares to venture out of the safety of her home.

She has also found it difficult to carry out her household chores and experiences a continuous sense of 'apprehension' that she is going to 'break down'. She claims that she only manages to keep going for the sake of the children.

The problem began fifteen months previously – three weeks after the birth of her second baby. She gradually became conscious that every time she was closed in by a crowd she grew extremely tense and developed pains in her head, neck and shoulders. Some time afterwards, she experienced her first panic attack at the checkout of the supermarket. It seemed to come 'out of the blue' and her immediate response was to run out of the store, leaving all her shopping still in her trolley. Once home, she felt both foolish and embarrassed by what she had done and decided not to return to that particular supermarket in case anyone recognized her. However, she soon began to avoid other shops just in case it brought on an attack and then she started to feel nervous driving the car, travelling on a bus or standing in a queue at the bank, or anywhere she felt 'trapped'. So worried by the possibility of having a panic attack did Lyn become, that she eventually became almost imprisoned in her own home. She feels guilty and ashamed because she thinks that she is not fulfilling her role as wife/mother and is eternally grateful that she is lucky enough to have a patient and understanding husband.

The people mentioned in these samples are typical of clients we have seen. They demonstrate several key features which will be noted and expanded in this book. Perhaps the outstanding point which should be noted at the outset is that they are all quite ordinary people; they are not 'mad' or 'mentally ill'. Although the symptoms they are experiencing may appear overwhelming at times, they are feelings which all of us have probably experienced at one time or another. Pat, Bill and Lyn are no different from most people reading this book.

Chapter 1

Anxiety: nature and extent

Fear and anxiety are emotions which everyone can recognize, and which everyone has experienced. Because these feelings are so widespread and commonplace they can be considered to be entirely normal reactions to certain events or situations. The terms 'fear' and 'anxiety' are often used interchangeably, and indeed they are used to describe the same kind of emotion. Although the distinction between the two is often blurred, Marks (1978a) has suggested that *anxiety* is used to describe an unpleasant feeling associated with impending danger which is not obvious to an onlooker. On the other hand, *fear* is seen as normal response to a perfectly realistic danger or threat. Although there may, on occasion, be some value in distinguishing fear and anxiety, the terms are often used synonymously; since the theory, assessment and treatment of both have substantial overlaps, no distinction will be maintained in this book.

Most people have experienced anxiety, and most of them would agree that it is an unpleasant feeling, yet surprisingly there is no completely satisfactory definition of what anxiety actually is. This has not, however, prevented the development of a number of theories of anxiety, some of which will be discussed in Chapter 4. One of the difficulties in defining anxiety stems from the range of phenomena which the term is used to cover. However, it is becoming accepted that three broad components of anxiety can be distinguished.

The three-systems model

Physiological arousal

This aspect of anxiety is produced by the activity of the autonomic nervous system, and is often referred to as 'somatic anxiety'. Individuals can be extremely aware of this component and will recognize such features as palpitations, perspiring and churning of the stomach. These features are fairly gross, and often much smaller changes can be monitored by using special recording methods to measure such things as blood pressure, respiration, muscle tension and various other physiological indices of arousal. An anxiety response does not usually show itself in a simple way through only one of these channels. While arousal can be detected in most response systems, it is likely that there will be more reaction in some systems than in others. Each individual's anxiety response may appear in a different way (Lacey 1967), and the predominant responses will only come to light after monitoring many channels.

Cognitive factors

These factors might also be called the subjective component of anxiety, since they refer to the feelings experienced by an individual. Someone might thus report feeling terrified, having a sense of dread, or feeling insecure.

There is another sense in which these factors can be described, and this refers to the thoughts that an individual has when approaching a situation or event which is expected to evoke some anxiety. The anxious person will likely be generating 'inner speech' or 'self-statements' describing the forthcoming event and the possible outcomes. In people prone to anxiety these statements will probably be negative in tone and will anticipate a negative outcome. Some examples of such statements are 'I can't go into that shop because it's crowded – even if I do, I will feel faint and I might pass out – I'll make a fool of myself and no-one will be able to help me – I can't do it – let me get out of here.' Statements such as these may be responsible for maintaining the whole anxiety response to some situations (Meichenbaum 1977).

Behavioural component

This feature of anxiety focuses on the overt, observable changes in behaviour. It may occur as a consequence of physiological arousal and would include such things as hand-wringing and fidgeting movements. At a more general level, the behavioural component describes attempts to escape from or avoid situations or objects which are likely to generate anxiety. Once such avoidance has been established, it can become extremely difficult to overcome.

This is a description of what has become known as the 'three systems' model of anxiety. The importance of the model lies in the fact that anxiety is no longer seen as an entity or a single system, but rather as a group of components which may be only loosely coupled together (Lang 1970). The three components are the cognitive, behavioural and physiological aspects of anxiety, but these components do not always correlate well with each other and often seem to be partially independent. Rachman and Hodgson (1974) have suggested the terms 'synchrony' and 'desynchrony' to describe changes in fear and avoidance which either vary together (synchrony) or vary independently or inversely (desynchrony). A further study (Hodgson and Rachman 1974) has attempted to establish the extent to which synchrony and desynchrony are subject to general rules or laws, and a search of the behaviour therapy literature led them to formulate certain hypotheses. They have suggested that synchrony or desynchrony among the three response systems may be a function of such factors as the intensity of emotional arousal or motivational factors. Other factors may relate to experimental variables such as the type of therapeutic intervention, length of follow-up, and the specific physiological system which is measured.

The three-systems model has provided new insights into the theory of anxiety, as well as promising possible new approaches to treatment (Rachman 1978a). However,

Hugdahl (1981) has warned that it may be unrealistic to expect the model to contribute to our understanding of anxiety without first defining very carefully the three components. For example, the 'cognitive component' may be taken to mean: (a) perception and labelling of autonomic arousal; (b) displaying anticipatory anxiety and negative cognitive rehearsal; or (c) changes in mood and feelings of unreality, guilt, self-blame, etc, when exposed to a phobic stimulus. More generally, Hugdahl suggests that we may have to reconsider what is meant by fear itself, since it is theoretically possible for three 'snake phobics' to display three different responses (behavioural, cognitive, physiological) to the same stimulus. Hugdahl wonders whether all three can reasonably be said to have the same fear, and notes the difficulty in comparing the intensity of fear across the three modalities.

The three-systems model may have implications for the aetiology of fear. Hugdahl speculates on a possible link between the pathway of fear acquisition and the response components involved. For example, a conditioning experience may produce physiological and behavioural responses, whereas in those fears acquired vicariously, the cognitive aspect might be predominant. While citing some preliminary evidence for this speculation, he admits that the data are far from conclusive. Finally, he welcomes the possibility of matching treatment method to the individual's fear response profile, suggesting that cognitive therapies might be most appropriate for those clients with large amounts of subjective anticipatory worry, whereas those with high physiological arousal might be best offered some relaxation-based method, such as systematic desensitization.

Hugdahl has produced an interesting and highly speculative examination of the three-systems model. However, until more detailed evidence is available, judgement of the utility of the model has to be deferred, although its promise must be acknowledged.

It is easy to form the impression that anxiety is a wholly maladaptive emotion. Nevertheless, the experience of anxiety is a fundamental response to a wide range of events and is a perfectly normal adaptation to various environmental circumstances. When we are faced with situations which threaten us and require us quickly to adjust our behaviour, the autonomic nervous system responds by producing a rise in blood pressure, an increase in respiration rate, a higher heart rate, and improved blood flow to the skeletal muscles. Physiologically, this is the same response as takes place during an anxiety attack. In a threatening situation, however, the response is nature's way of preparing the body for conflict or escape, and this apparently innate 'fight or flight' reaction is evident in many species as well as in humans. In an evolutionary sense, it can be seen that the members of a species with the most keenly developed 'fight or flight' responses had a better chance of survival, and hence increased their probability of reproducing. Everyone is prone to such a reaction, and it is a perfectly normal occurrence; it is when this reaction occurs in the absence of an occasion demanding fight or flight that it becomes abnormal and is labelled anxiety.

Anxiety is also held to be abnormal when it occurs to a much greater degree than is usual for most people. For example, many people might feel mildly anxious when having to speak in public, but the level is not such that it causes them to avoid doing so.

Thus it may be seen that anxiety is defined or labelled as abnormal or a problem by reference to either its *intensity* (i.e. it is more severe than the stimulus warrants) or the *context* in which it occurs (i.e. there is no objective threat in the situation to account for the subjective experience).

The extent of the problem

Estimating how widespread and how severe a problem anxiety is in society today is not a simple matter. It is complicated by a number of factors related to problems of defining anxiety. Unlike many physical illnesses, anxiety cannot be diagnosed by a simple test. Anxiety is primarily defined on a subjective basis and the degree to which a person suffers before labelling the state abnormal and seeking help, will vary between individuals. Thus the point at which 'normal' anxiety merges into 'abnormal' is not only determined by severity but by many other factors such as individual level of tolerance, the situation in which it occurs and the rationality of the experience. As an example, take the person who is just about to take a driving test. A rapid heart beat, sweaty hands and feeling of fear and dread may be perceived as a normal reaction to the situation. Experiencing the same feelings when entering a local post office is a far less normal state of affairs.

Assessing the prevalence of anxiety is further complicated by the fact that it is also found to be associated with, or an exacerbating factor in, a large number of other conditions. Examples are depression, irritability, sleep disturbance, headaches, reduced libido, asthma, stomach upsets and many more. Moreover, it may be a *transitory* state in reaction to a real situation such as sitting examinations, starting a new job, or a *chronic* social and health problem. Finally, the consequences are manifold; there is the immediate personal discomfort, the development of maladaptive behaviour patterns and sometimes a longer-term process such as the development of heart disease.

It can be appreciated that because anxiety is an umbrella term it is difficult to obtain specific data on prevalence. The best source of information we have about the prevalence of anxiety and related complaints in the general population comes from surveys of consultation patterns in general practice. Although this does not give a complete picture because some people will seek help elsewhere (for example, friends, clergymen, Samaritans, self-help groups, etc), it is the case that nearly everyone is registered with a family doctor and research has indicated that the vast majority would use this service first when ill.

One of the most extensive research studies on the prevalence of psychiatric morbidity in the community is by Michael Shepherd and his colleagues at the London Institute of Psychiatry. This is a survey started in the 1950s of 46 general practices in London (Shepherd *et al.* 1966). The population sample was chosen because it is representative of Greater London for demographic and social characteristics. However, it is less certain how representative Greater London is of the rest of the country. This survey established that psychiatric disorder is a major contributor to chronic illness at the general-practice level. Out of the 'at risk' population examined, 13 per cent consulted with a psychiatric problem, a consultation rate exceeded only by respiratory disorders. Although this figure includes all psychiatric states, the majority recorded fell into the 'neurotic' category in which anxiety is the predominant feature.

The second national study carried out in 1970–71 by the Royal College of General Practitioners (1974) based on data from 53 practices throughout the country, found that 12 per cent of consultations were for psychiatric reasons. In the Shepherd survey, the inter-practice variation showed a ninefold difference between the highest and lowest rate of patients consulting for psychiatric reasons. These differences may be put down to a number of factors such as recording errors, fluctuation associated with random sampling and even true differences in prevalence according to social/ geographical variables. Perhaps the most significant influences are to do with doctors' attitudes and diagnostic habits. Doctors tend to accumulate certain types of patients according to special interests and aptitudes. The 'selective recruitment' will therefore contribute to true inter-practice differences. A more serious hindrance to obtaining accurate figures is that doctors perceive symptoms differently. They vary in their predisposition to see complaints primarily as organic or functional and hence the diagnostic label they would attach to each individual will vary accordingly. This is particularly a problem in cases of complaints with mixed organic and functional origins, such as asthma, which may be over- or under-included according to the general practitioner's predilections. This factor is further complicated by the tendency of patients to present initially with somatic complaints regardless of eventual diagnosis.

Nevertheless, in summary, although there are some problems with interpreting the data, evidence such as it is indicates that anxiety and its associated complaints are a common problem and one with which the family doctor is frequently faced.

Anxiety and other problems

It is important to draw attention to the fact that as well as the direct consequences of anxiety, such as personal discomfort, impairment of performance and so forth, there are also longer-term, indirect consequences. The role of anxiety in learned avoidance patterns has been well researched, and problems such as agoraphobia may lead to social withdrawal, depression, work problems and marital breakdown.

The person suffering from anxiety may experience many handicaps at work. He or she may be overly affected by the ordinary stresses and pressures of employment associated with a demanding workload, or have a low tolerance for factors such as high noise levels or boredom with repetitive tasks. There may also be social difficulties related to developing good working relationships with colleagues and making friends. These problems, combined with low self-esteem, may diminish promotion prospects and result in under-achievement. Time may be lost through an abnormal degree of psychosomatic illnesses or through incapacities brought about by phobias. For these and other causes the anxious individual may either experience a reduced job satisfaction or in extreme cases job loss or inability to gain employment. It has been estimated that 37 million working days in the UK are lost per year through psychological disorder, which considerably exceeds the 23 million days lost through accidents at work (Sims 1983), and it may be suggested that a large proportion of psychological problems accounting for this figure have an anxiety-related component.

Loss of job, or reduced performance and associated pressures, may in time have an adverse effect in other areas of the individual's life. Marital and social relationship difficulties are another area where anxiety may play a prominent part. Social fears such as anxiety about going into public places, pubs, shops and so forth may serve to severely limit an individual's access to friends and leisure activities. Lowered self-esteem may lead to an inability to cope with the usual domestic demands of home and family and excessive dependence on a partner within the marriage. This in itself may cause a build-up of frustration and resentment between partners and ultimately put unacceptable strains on family relationships. This may be compounded by other aspects of anxiety such as irritability, insomnia, lowered libido and feelings of guilt.

Disruption of work and family patterns in some cases leads the individual to seek solace in maladaptive forms of coping such as drug or alcohol abuse. These may form part of an attempt of 'self-medication', for example, the use of alcohol or sedatives as a means of lowering subjective anxiety and tension. Having a drink to 'calm one's nerves' is a commonly used aid in our society, but if it becomes a necessity to drink to face the daily stresses of living the anxious person is in danger of compounding the first problem with a second, namely alcoholism.

Anxiety and tension have been identified as components of the Type A personality, which has been linked with higher than average rates of heart disease (Rosenman *et al.* 1975). Type A behaviour is described by Suinn and Bloom (1978) as 'an intense drive towards self selected but poorly defined goals, difficulty in relaxing, accentuation of words in normal speech, aggressive competitiveness and a sense of time urgency'. These authors have produced an 'anxiety management training' package which has been used with some success in stress management.

From the foregoing discussion it can be seen that efforts to determine the extent of the problem of anxiety in the general population have to take into account a far wider array of complaints than may initially be labelled as anxiety, so it is with some justification that anxiety may be claimed to be a

major cause of distress in the general population requiring
the intervention of the helping professions.

Chapter 2

Anxiety: clinical aspects and problems

Anxiety states

While some people can link their fears and anxieties to specific events and circumstances, the majority of those who have anxiety problems find that they feel anxious for no obvious reason. This is known as an *anxiety state*, and at its worst the person suffers from an almost continuous feeling of anxiety or tension, which may only recede for very short periods at a time. There is a general restlessness and irritability which is often accompanied by feelings of near constant tiredness and lack of energy. It is usual that the person feels that something dreadful is about to happen, and so is frequently apprehensive about the future. However, when pushed, the person is usually unable to be specific about what is actually feared; there is instead a marked vagueness about the future. In fact, forcing someone to be specific about what they fear may cause the worry to subside temporarily, since they will be unlikely to pinpoint anything they really need to worry about. In addition to what amounts to a chronic state of tension and mild anxiety, the person may be subject to acute, terrifying bouts of panic which do not appear to be linked to anything the individual is doing at the time, and are often described as 'coming out of the blue'. These episodes typically last a few minutes but can vary considerably and in some cases may last an hour or more. However long they last objectively, to the sufferer they may seem like an eternity. During these times a range of both somatic and cognitive symptoms may be experienced. These may include palpitations, dizziness, tightness in the chest, feelings of choking, trembling hands, wobbly legs, and a general feeling of being unwell. Breathing may seem difficult, or someone may overbreathe to the extent that it produces tingling sensations in the arms and legs. People often wonder what is happening to them, and a common thought is that they are having a heart attack or some other serious physical trouble. Perhaps the major disturbing feature of these panic attacks is their apparent un-predictability. This uncertainty may play havoc with a person's life, since he or she may avoid a wide range of activities, lest they trigger one of their 'turns'. The degree of incapacity can be quite substantial, leading to severe restrictions on the individual's lifestyle. On the other hand, there are those who complain of feeling anxious most of the time, but who try to ignore this as best they can and not allow it to interfere with their activities at all.

It is not uncommon for anxiety sufferers, especially those who are prone to panic attacks, to have been sent to general hospitals or to casualty departments where they have been thoroughly examined by physicians, and have been given a wide range of tests for various physical problems, all of which turn out to be negative. By a process of elimination, one illness after another is gradually ruled out, and in the absence of any detectable physical cause for the 'funny turn' the next port of call may be to see a psychiatrist or a psychologist. A person may initially be reluctant to accept that anxiety or tension may be responsible for the peculiar experiences they have had, since this can suggest to them that they are in some way mentally unstable with all the stigma that such a label carries. Some never find themselves able to accept a psychological explanation of their symptoms, and seek frequent appointments with their general practitioners to be reassured that they do not have heart trouble or another disease.

Anxiety states are conditions in which the anxiety does not

have a particular focus. On the other hand, if a fear is highly specific, is triggered by a particular situation and has a debilitating effect on a person's life it is called a *phobia*. Many people have irrational fears or even simply dislikes which they call phobias; it is probably best to reserve the term for those fears which make a significant impact on a person's life. In all phobias, the degree of fear experienced is completely disproportionate to the situation and limits the person's lifestyle to a considerable extent. It is possible that phobias may develop to almost any situation, although there is evidence that there are some situations or objects for which people are much more likely to develop phobias than others. This is a point of considerable theoretical interest, and will be discussed in relation to some of the explanations of fear which are covered in Chapter 4.

Agoraphobia

The most common phobia which is seen in hospitals and clinics is agoraphobia. The term is derived from the Greek word *agora* which means a market place.[1] Thus the term agoraphobia quite literally means fear of the market place, or to substitute the modern equivalent, fear of shopping areas or precincts and other busy areas. There is a common misconception that the word refers to a fear of open spaces, but although it is true that some agoraphobic people find it difficult to venture outside the house, a fear of open spaces is not the primary feature of the disorder.

There is no discrete 'cause' of the problem, in that it reliably follows from a particular incident, or series of incidents. However, reports from agoraphobic individuals suggest that the problem develops following such major life

[1]Some years ago it was fashionable to give phobias impressive names, usually derived from Latin or Greek, e.g. arachnephobia (fear of spiders), orphidiophobia (fear of snakes) and acrophobia (fear of heights). However, there is little to commend this tendency; it merely substitutes a more impressive name for a less impressive one, adding nothing to description, explanation or treatment. Happily it has virtually disappeared.

events as childbirth, moving house, becoming married, becoming divorced, serious physical illness or the death of someone close. Indeed, any major change in circumstances may precede the onset of agoraphobia, but it would not be justified to say that such an event in itself was responsible for the development of the disorder.

A range of fears is included under the general heading of agoraphobia, and it may make more sense to talk of the 'agoraphobic syndrome' than to imply that there is one specific phobia. Typically, the kinds of things an agoraphobia sufferer finds difficult will include travelling by public transport (yet travelling by car or taxi may present no difficulty), going to the theatre or cinema or visiting the shops. If a visit to the cinema is attempted, a seat will be chosen at the end of a row rather than in the middle, so that a speedy 'escape' can be made if necessary. Visits to the hairdresser are also difficult, and again the victim may feel 'trapped' when sitting under the hair-dryer. Shops may vary in the amount of difficulty they present to the agoraphobic person. The general rule is that the larger the shop, the more anxiety will be provoked; indeed, supermarkets are often singled out as being particularly difficult places in which to keep calm. In places such as those mentioned, agoraphobic people will begin to feel hot, flustered and may experience all the features of an acute panic attack such as palpitations, sweating, shakiness, dizziness, etc. At the same time, a number of thoughts may come to mind such as 'Am I having a heart attack?' or 'I'm going to faint and look foolish'. The physical symptoms and the thoughts will develop to such a pitch that the person will eventually try to flee from the situation so as to relieve the fear and possible embarrassment. In fact, when agoraphobic people are asked about the worst aspect of a panic attack, a frequent reply is that they are afraid of looking foolish in front of others, and they regard the possibility of fainting in public as embarrassing in the extreme. These supposed social consequences of the panic attack are often foremost in the sufferer's mood, and may take precedence over concerns about physical wellbeing.

In very severe cases of agoraphobia, the person may hardly manage to venture out of the house and reach the front gate without experiencing a panic attack. His or her home may be the only place where someone with severe agoraphobia feels safe. The presence of another person will often be sufficient to allow the agoraphobic to venture into the feared situations. Some sufferers become so anxious that they ensure that someone from the immediate family circle is at home with them most of the day, and will be 'on call' should they need to venture out at all. It is not unknown for the spouse of an agoraphobic individual to be telephoned at work and then implored to return home at once to pacify a panicking partner.

In some cases, the agoraphobic may not need another person to be present when venturing outside but can derive sufficient comfort from having something to do such as pushing a pram, walking a dog, or having something to carry. Going out after dark is often easier than during the day and a number of people find it helpful to wear dark glasses if going out in daytime. These 'props' can sometimes make all the difference between being able to go out to a certain place or not. Without them, the anxiety may be so severe that any movement is greatly restricted. An example will illustrate the degree of severity that can occur.

Eileen was a 39-year-old shop manager, happily married but with no family. Around 18 months previously, she had had a severe bout of 'flu which had meant that she was off work for several weeks, staying in bed most of the time. She had returned to work only for a day or two when she experienced a sudden feeling of panic while in the middle of her store. She reported palpitations, a churning stomach, general shakiness and a feeling that she was about to collapse. She had two further episodes during that week, and had returned home earlier than usual. Over the next month or so Eileen had further panic attacks when shopping in the supermarket, at the post office and in church as well as at her place of work. She became increasingly fearful of venturing outside, and would spend her weekends entirely indoors.

After another few months she was unwilling to go to work and began to stay at home all the time. As soon as she stepped outside she felt generally apprehensive that 'something might happen' although she could not be more specific; if she forced herself to go out, she would invariably experience a panic attack. Just before she was referred to the clinic, she had become afraid even to venture out of her own bedroom in the morning, and would only make brief visits to the kitchen to collect some food which she would take back to the bedroom to eat. Her GP, who had to visit her at home, convinced her to attend the clinic, and although reluctant initially, eventually agreed to be taken there by her husband, and treatment was able to begin.

Specific phobias

Apart from the cluster of phobic items associated with the agoraphobic syndrome, the other main types of phobias can be classed as fears relating to illness, and fears relating to social situations.

Illness phobias

Most people will have entertained a fear of illness at some time or other, and it can be said that to do so is entirely normal. An illness phobia, on the other hand, is a morbid fear of a specific illness in an otherwise healthy person. It is usually possible to distinguish an illness phobia from hypochondriasis, since the phobia is typically concerned with one particular illness, where the hypochondriac tends to worry about health in general and the illness in question may change quite regularly.

There is one key aspect that distinguishes illness phobias from others; in most phobias it is possible to avoid the phobic object, or to escape from it if contact has been made inadvertently. However, the person who worries about being the victim of an illness or disease has no method of escaping from this persistent and unwelcome thought. The method of relieving anxiety which tends to be used most is to seek the reassurance of another person. In many cases, this reassurance can be provided by a relative or friend, but in more extreme cases, the 'victim' will only be satisfied by consulting a medical practitioner. Such people frequently consult their family doctors, but occasionally they request that they be sent to a hospital so that they can have the opinion of a specialist. An example follows.

Alan was a 44-year-old married teacher who was terrified that he might develop a brain tumour. He could remember always being a little over-concerned about matters of health, but three years previously a parent of one of his pupils had died from a brain tumour. From that time Alan had focused all his health concerns on the possibility that he too might develop a similar tumour. This fear had reached the point where it was almost constantly on his mind, and was affecting his teaching. He was unable to prepare his lessons properly, and at weekends and holidays he had taken to sitting around the house worrying all the while that he might have a tumour. He would not read a newspaper for fear that he might learn about someone who had died of a brain tumour or any other cancer, and he would not allow the television or radio to be switched on at news time for the same reason. He had tried to talk the matter over with his wife, who made numerous attempts to reassure him. He was unwilling, however, to talk to his GP about the problem, but eventually he was persuaded to do so, and as a result further help was arranged.

Social phobias

Social phobias often centre around worries about eating or drinking in the presence of others. Sufferers usually fear that their hands will shake and tremble, that they will drop the cup they are holding or that they will blush, or become conspicuous to others. Writing with someone else looking on, e.g. when signing a cheque, may also trigger similar worries. The more formal the occasion, the worse the fear will be, and it can have a crippling effect on the person's life.

An office worker may not be able to hand cups of tea to the boss and a young man may feel unable to take tea with his fiancée's parents.

Much of the fear is in anticipation of what might happen when the dreaded event occurs and this worrying in advance can be worse than the actual fear experienced at the time. The degree of shaking or trembling which may take place might only be noticeable to the sufferer, and would appear almost non-existent to the objective outsider. Nevertheless, the problem remains every bit as severe, even when its 'internal' nature is acknowledged. An example of a social phobia is given below.

Janice was a 29-year-old assistant social worker who was terrified of eating or drinking in the presence of others. When she attempted to do so, she worried that her hands would shake and that she would drop the cup or the cutlery she was holding. The problem had begun when she was in her mid-teens; she was one of a group of teenagers in a café, and also in the group was a boy she was very keen on. As she reached for her cup, she became aware that this boy was looking at her, and as she looked back at him, she found she was spilling her coffee into the saucer. She became greatly embarrassed at this, blushed, and left the café. Subsequently she found that she became apprehensive of having a drink with other people present, and this also generalized to eating with others. The problem developed over the years, and at the time of her first interview at the clinic, she had not eaten or had a drink with anyone outside her immediate family for over five years. Indeed, even at home she would only use mugs (she worried that rattling a cup and saucer would draw unwelcome attention to her), and would only use a knife and fork in front of her husband. If other family were present she would restrict herself to eating sandwiches or cakes, or else would make the excuse that she had a poor appetite and was not hungry. All these problems existed despite the fact that her husband had assured her on numerous occasions that he was unable to detect any substantial degree of shaking in her hands.

Phobias of specific events or objects

Other phobias may be highly specific to discrete situations but may have an extremely disruptive effect on the sufferer's husband or wife.

Mary was a 29-year-old woman who was terrified of thunderstorms. Her problems could be traced back to around the time when she was six years old. She had had her photograph taken and was frightened by the flash (and in fact had not posed for a photograph since). From that time she was generally uneasy during thunderstorms, but five years ago, a severe storm resulted in the ground floor of her house being flooded. Since then, she had become increasingly frightened at the prospect of a thunderstorm. She read all weather forecasts in the newspapers, listened to all available weather information on radio and TV, studied the 'Teletext' pages on the weather, and telephoned the local meteorological station several times a day. She became quite agitated at the sight of a dark cloud, and even in sunny weather she felt apprehensive that it might end in a thunderstorm. Some weeks before coming to the clinic, there had been a series of blizzards over a period of a fortnight, and she had been so worried by these that she had lost nearly a stone in weight. Any change in the weather made her so anxious that she would plead with her husband not to go to work, but to stay at home with her, which he had done on a number of occasions over the past year.

Obsessive-compulsive disorders

Such problems are usually distinguished from phobias and they are characterized by the persistent occurrence of an unwanted, often distressing thought which comes to mind despite every effort to resist it. These thoughts are often to do with anxiety about contamination or possible harm that might occur to another person. The thoughts may or may not be accompanied by a morbid, irresistible urge to perform a certain action which is usually repetitive in nature. However, its performance may reduce subjective feelings of anxiety and preventing the action usually leads to an increase in anxiety. This sort of behaviour is quite commonplace in childhood, and is an accepted part of development. Most of us will be able to recall trying to avoid stepping on cracked paving stones or having to touch every other lamppost with some imagined dire consequence if we failed in our task. Sometimes it may not be necessary to indulge in an explicit action, and instead it may be that a certain series of thoughts have to be brought into mind, or that a particular object has to be stared at so that its precise form may be recalled at a future date.

Rituals and ruminations can take many forms, and may include such things as checking light switches and plugs over and over again to ensure that they are off, or taking an inordinately long time to get dressed or to wash after having visited the lavatory. Almost any routine, everyday task can become the focus of rituals or ruminations, and these simple matters which most of us can perform in seconds or minutes can take on mammoth proportions for the obsessional individual and may take them many hours to complete.

For example, *Brenda* was a 28-year-old teacher whose problems began after a health inspector had laid down poison to kill rats at her school. This caused a certain smell about the school which Brenda associated with dead rats and with germs. Around the same time she started to visit a hospital every week as a volunteer. Before she went on her hospital rounds she would clean herself thoroughly, wash her hair, and change her clothes, since she was afraid of spreading infection to the patients. This progressed until she reached the stage where she had to have separate clothes to wear at home and at school. She also became afraid of dirty laundry of any kind, but especially if she could not be certain who had used it, and would handle it only with rubber gloves. After this she would scrape her nails into a bar of soap and scrub for ten minutes or more to ensure they were clean. If she tried to stop the handwashing, things would become worse and she would become very tense, and agitated. She washed virtually everything she touched –

clothes, crockery, herself and anything around the house. She had the same problems at school where she would avoid touching objects which other people had touched such as door handles, and would try to wash and disinfect herself if she accidentally touched such an item. At home, her husband was spending most of his time washing clothes for her, and he himself ended up, on her instructions, washing his own hands many times. In the end she thought that he too was contaminated and eventually would not allow him to enter the room she was in.

Chapter 3

The measurement of anxiety

There are two main reasons why people are interested in measuring anxiety. Research workers who are concerned with developing theories about the phenomenon are interested in looking at the nature of 'normal anxiety', for example, examining individual differences in arousal levels or degree of responsivity in different physiological systems. Clinicians are primarily interested in measuring anxiety as a means of judging the effectiveness of specific clinical interventions, for example, the response of a group of people to a new method of treatment or at an individual level as a means of evaluating progress over the course of treatment.

The complex, multi-modal nature of anxiety, which has been discussed in earlier chapters, is reflected in the various techniques of measurement that have been developed. For discussion purposes these will be grouped into three broad categories:

1. Self-report measures
2. Behavioural observations
3. Physiological recordings.

These measures cannot be viewed as equivalent, in so far as changes measured by one method are not necessarily to be found in the others. Again, this reflects the poor correlation between cognitive, behavioural and physiological aspects of anxiety. Furthermore, there are variations in both the sensitivity and the specificity of these assessment tools, which will be noted in the following descriptions.

Self-report measures

Self-report data are perhaps the most widely used method of evaluating treatment outcome, and a broad range of rating scales, questionnaires, and checklists have been devised. These scales differ according to the degree of specificity of the situation to which the anxiety response is being measured.

1. Questionnaires with rating scales

A number of questionnaires have been devised comprising of a list of diverse statements related to subjective feeling states, which the respondent has to rate according to a given scale. The Self-Evaluation Questionnaire developed by Spielberger, Gorsuch and Lushene (1970) is a typical example. (See Table 3.1 for examples of both forms of this scale.) The respondent is required to consider a list of 20 statements such as those shown in Table 3.1, and to rate each one on a four-point intensity scale. This scale is designed to assess the level of 'state anxiety', or the particular level of anxiety experienced at that moment. State anxiety is described as 'a transitory emotional state or condition of the human organism that is characterized by subjective consciously perceived feelings of tension and apprehension, and heightened autonomic nervous system activity'. In other words, state anxiety may vary from moment to moment and may be triggered by the situation one is facing. An example of state anxiety is the type of feeling most of us might have immediately before sitting a driving test. There is a parallel form of the questionnaire (STAI-X2) in which a similar list of statements is rated according to how the respondent feels generally by using a frequency scale, viz. 'almost never – sometimes – often – almost always'. This is designed to measure 'trait anxiety' defined by the authors as 'anxiety proneness' which

Table 3.1 Some sample items from the state-trait anxiety inventory*

STAI FORM X-1

NAME _____ DATE _____

DIRECTIONS: A number of statements which people
have used to describe themselves are given below.
Read each statement and then blacken in the
appropriate circle to the right of the statement to indicate how you *feel* right now, that
is, *at this moment*. There are no right or
wrong answers. Do not spend too much time
on any one statement but give the answer
which seems to describe your present
feelings best.

	Not at all	Somewhat	Moderately so	Very much so
1. I feel calm	①	②	③	④
2. I feel secure	①	②	③	④
3. I am tense	①	②	③	④
4. I am regretful	①	②	③	④
5. I feel at ease	①	②	③	④

STAI FORM X-2

NAME _____ DATE _____

DIRECTIONS: A number of statements which people
have used to describe themselves are given below.
Read each statement and then blacken in the
appropriate circle to the right of the statement to indicate how you *generally* feel. There
are no right or wrong answers. Do not spend too
much time on any one statement but give the
answer which seems to describe how you generally feel.

	Almost never	Sometimes	Often	Almost always
21. I feel pleasant	①	②	③	④
22. I tire quickly	①	②	③	④
23. I feel like crying	①	②	③	④
24. I wish I could be as happy as others seem to be	①	②	③	④
25. I am losing out on things because I can't make up my mind soon enough	①	②	③	④

*Source: The State Trait Anxiety Inventory, 1967, 1983.

is relatively stable over time. It is trait anxiety that one is referring to when we say that someone is 'a general worrier'. In other words, it describes a tendency to be anxious for much of the time, regardless of the particular situation which exists at any one moment.

The Taylor Manifest Anxiety Scale (Taylor 1953) is another example. This comprises a wide-ranging list of feeling states, e.g. 'I am a very nervous person'; questions related to general health, e.g. 'I have a great deal of stomach trouble'; and actual behavioural tendencies e.g. 'I cry easily'. These are marked simply true or false, and the overall score obtained by an individual can be compared against a standardization sample. A similar scale is the General Health Questionnaire (Goldberg 1972) in which a series of questions related to the respondent's general health over the past few weeks are rated on a four-point frequency scale, e.g.:

Have you recently been having hot and cold spells?	Not at all	No more than usual	Rather more than usual	Much more than usual

This questionnaire covers a wider range than just anxiety-related symptoms. The present authors have developed a simple anxiety symptom checklist which they have used as an outcome measure in clinical research. This differs from the above measures in so far as it concentrates on physical symptomatology rather than generalized subjective conditions. It was derived in the following way. Firstly, a study was made of all letters received by the Psychology Department in a small urban teaching hospital over a three-month period, referring clients for treatment of anxiety. Every symptom described in these letters was included in the checklist. Secondly, all interviews of clients who had been seen in the Psychology Department over a six-month period for management of their anxiety were examined, and descriptions of symptoms were noted. Any symptoms not previously recorded in the referral letters were added to the checklist. The total number of symptoms derived from these procedures was 77. Each symptom was rated on a five-point scale on which a subject indicated the severity of that symptom. The example given in Table 3.2 will give an illustration.

Table 3.2 Some sample items from the Rowan Anxiety Symptom Checklist

NAME ————————————————— DATE ————

Below is a list of symptoms which people can experience. Please indicate which ones bother you, and also how much of a problem it is by ticking the appropriate line.

	Not a problem	Slightly trouble-some	Moder-ately trouble-some	Very trouble-some	A severe problem
1. Tightness in chest					
2. Irritability					
3. Lack of confidence					
4. Sleeplessness					
5. Being short of breath					

2. Fear survey schedules

These are measures of phobic anxiety and differ from the above scales in that subjects are presented with a list of a wide variety of specific objects or situations and asked to estimate the degree of fear each situation would arouse on a five- or seven-point scale. Thus, whereas in the questionnaire rating scales the focus is on the subjective report of anxiety generally and over time, in the fear survey schedules the

Table 3.3 An example of a Fear Survey Schedule

| NAME | | | | DATE |

The items in this questionnaire are things that many ordinary people are afraid of. Please tick one of the columns opposite each item to indicate how much each item bothers you.

	Not at all	A little	A fair amount	A lot	Very much
1. Crowded places	____	____	____	____	____
2. Spiders	____	____	____	____	____
3. Travelling alone by bus	____	____	____	____	____
4. The sight of blood	____	____	____	____	____
5. Flyovers	____	____	____	____	____
6. Eating or drinking with other people	____	____	____	____	____

focus is on the external stimuli. An example is given in Table 3.3. Versions of fear survey schedules have been developed by Geer (1965), Wolpe and Lang (1964) and Braun and Reynolds (1969). They differ in the number of items, whether they have been empirically derived and whether they are designed primarily as research or clinical instruments. When used as research tools their main use has been in screening a population to identify phobic individuals. Their main clinical use has been to uncover fears experienced by clients which may bear relevance to the presenting problem.

3. Specific measures

Some scales have been developed which address themselves to specific situational fears and contain a number of questions relating to particular objects or aspects of a situation. Examples of such scales are the Lang, Melamed and Hart (1970) scales measuring fear of snakes or spiders, and the Suinn Test Anxiety Behaviour Scale (STABS) developed by Suinn (1969). These scales are very similar in layout to the Fear Survey Schedules described above. However, instead of listing a range of separate items, they list many examples of the same basic fear. These may be of use to the clinician since they may help to establish a hierarchy for desensitization (see Ch. 5).

4. Self-monitoring scales

The preceding anxiety measures, while providing a general overall assessment of an individual's feeling state at any one time, prove to be less sensitive to change over time than is frequently needed for clinical monitoring purposes. Some-times, for example during relaxation training or exposure treatments, it is necessary to be able to monitor moment-to-moment changes in levels of fear. The most widely used method of assessing momentary changes in anxiety in relation to a specific stimulus is the 'fear thermometer' (Walk 1956). It usually has a ten-point scale with anchor points. A score of 1 denotes 'completely calm' and 10 is 'absolute terror'. Subjects are asked to rate their level of fear by marking an appropriate point on the scale. A similar technique is described by Wolpe and Lazarus (1966) where the individual gives a 'SUDS' rating (subjective units of distress). A slight variation on these self-monitoring scales is the Affect Adjective Checklist (AACL) developed by Zuckerman (1960), in which subjects tick off from a list the words which best describe how they feel at any given time. The state anxiety scale of the Spielberger Self-Evaluation Questionnaire can also be used in this manner.

There are a number of advantages to using questionnaire measures of anxiety. State anxiety measures may be used repeatedly in the clinical situation to monitor changes in levels of arousal, giving useful feedback on treatment progress. Another major advantage is the ease of administration of questionnaire measures – they do not require specialist knowledge or equipment to be used effectively. There is, however, one major drawback related to their validity. Some individuals may either over- or underestimate their level of reported anxiety in order perhaps to give responses that they think are in some sense desirable, which has the effect of either inflating or reducing the score.

Behavioural observations

Some of the criticisms aimed at self-report measures on the basis of their over-reliance on subjectivity are overcome by the use of observational measures of actual behaviour. This aspect of research and treatment is one of the hallmarks of the behavioural approach. Borkovec, Weerts and Bernstein (1977) distinguish two classes of behavioural observations, direct and indirect.

1. Direct observations

The direct assessment of anxiety focuses on the overt, observable effects of physiological events on behaviour, and the interfering effect that arousal has on performance. Instruments used to aid this assessment attempt to quantify the presence, the intensity or the frequency of overt signs of anxiety. A typical example of such an instrument was that developed by Paul (1966) to measure public-speaking anxiety. He constructed the Timed Behavioural Checklist which was used by trained observers to rate the performance of subjects while they gave a short speech before an audience. The observers noted the occurrence of such things as trembling hands, stammerings, throat clearings, foot shuffling, and quivering voice, using these to arrive at an index of anxiety.

More sophisticated methods have entailed the use of video-taped recording of an individual's performance. An obvious advantage of this method is that it provides a permanent record which can be reviewed, so both observer reliability can be double-checked and pre–post treatment comparisons made.

2. Indirect observations

The indirect assessment of anxiety involves measures of observable approach to or escape/avoidance of fear-provoking stimuli. The name usually given to this type of test is the Behavioural Avoidance Test (BAT). The intensity of anxiety is assessed by measuring how near to the feared object a person can approach or how long its presence can be tolerated. The BAT is probably the most widely used method and was first reported by Lang and Lazovik (1963). Snake-phobic subjects were asked to approach and, if possible, handle a caged snake. The test was administered before and after treatment and changes in approach behaviour were taken as indices of improvement.

The BAT is a useful measure when anxiety is related to a specific object or event, but is of little value if the anxiety is generalized. It has the main advantage of being objective and readily quantifiable. However, a valid criticism challenges it on the basis of 'artificiality'. Since it is usually conducted in a 'safe' environment such as a hospital or clinic, it may not necessarily be a valid predictor of behaviour under more natural conditions. For example, an individual may make a supreme effort to handle a spider for fear of appearing 'stupid' in front of others; however, his or her normal life may be severely disrupted, so as to avoid coming into contact with spiders even at a considerable distance.

Physiological recordings

The physiological activity that accompanies reports of anxiety has become a focus for much research. The theoretical models based on physiological indices are complex and beyond the scope of this volume. However, there are some reports of clinical uses of physiological recordings for both assessment and biofeedback purposes. A number of physiological indices have been studied including blood pressure, blood volume, respiration rate, heart rate and muscle tension. However, the two most widely researched response symptoms have been electrodermal activity and cardiac responses.

1. Electrodermal activity

It is generally accepted that skin resistance is directly related to activity in the sympathetic nervous system which innervates the sweat glands. Changes in psychological state can therefore be monitored by measuring skin resistance using electrode placements on the palms of the hands. The resistance level always decreases with increased arousal.

Individual differences in the level of skin resistance have been investigated as indices of fear and anxiety. Lader and Wing (1966) found that the resting levels of skin resistance were lower in clinically anxious individuals than in controls. However, it is questionable whether this relationship is a simple one, or as consistent or reliable as would be hoped. There is some evidence that fluctuations in skin resistance which occur spontaneously at different rates, may be a more simple and accurate index of arousal (Lick and Katkin 1976).

2. Muscle tension

This may be assessed by recording the action potentials from specific muscles – a procedure known as electromyography. Skin electrodes are placed at specific sites such as the forearm or forehead at a standard distance apart (see Fig. 3.1). The most frequent clinical use has been as part of a treatment programme using biofeedback methods for tension-related problems such as headaches.

3. Cardiac responses

The measurement of heart rate can be made extremely accurately using sophisticated and expensive apparatus such as the polygraph, or slightly less accurately, but much more cheaply, by taking a pulse from the wrist. This latter method has been used to good effect in a number of experiments on fear (e.g. Borkovec 1973).

Heart rate usually shows marked increases when people are confronted with fearful stimuli. The relationships

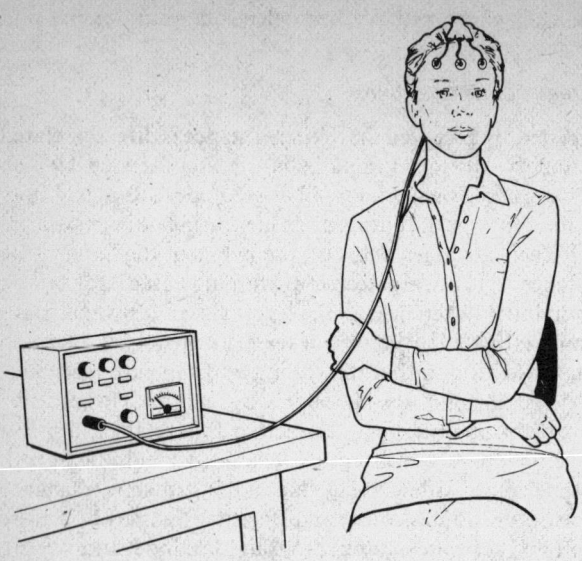

Fig. 3.1.

between changes in heart rate and stimulation are not always
straightforward, however, since heart rate is also responsive
to various perceptual and cognitive activities which may
interact with the arousal response (Borkovec *et al.* 1977).

Although physiological measures of anxiety have the
advantage of being relatively independent and objective,
there are a number of drawbacks. Technical difficulties can
make accurate, reliable recordings problematic and time
consuming; for example, fluctuations in ambient tempera-
ture, spurious movements and the presence of certain drugs
can all affect the recordings. The apparatus is usually
expensive and technically sophisticated, calling for specialized
knowledge to operate it and to interpret the results. Its use
tends to lie more in the area of experimental research than in

clinical outcome studies and since there is little correlation between physiological changes, changes in behaviour and in self-reported anxiety this will probably remain the case.

Chapter 4

Theories of anxiety

Various theories of fear acquisition and maintenance have been proposed, and for ease of discussion these have been divided broadly into the 'conditioning' and the 'non-conditioning' theories.

The conditioning theory

The classical conditioning model of anxiety can be traced to the writings of J. B. Watson (Watson and Rayner 1920) and his student, Mary Cover Jones (1924). They describe an early experimental approach to conditioning a fear of rats in an eleven-month-old boy, little Albert, and subsequent attempts to rid him of this fear.

It had been observed that Albert exhibited a marked emotional response when a steel bar was struck, producing a loud, unpleasant noise. He broke into a fit of crying. This noise was then associated with the white rat (previously not feared by Albert). The rat was presented to Albert and just as he was about to touch it the bar was struck behind his head. After several pairings of the rat with the noise, it was observed that the sight of the rat alone was sufficient to cause Albert to cry. This conditioned emotional response had been established by the contigual (close temporal) association of arousal with a previously neutral event (the rat). The same classical conditioning procedure was described in the famous experiments by Pavlov (1927) who conditioned dogs to salivate to the sound of a bell.

Watson viewed anxiety symptoms as conditioned emotional responses, the process of conditioning being entirely Pavlovian in nature. In general terms, the model states that if a previously neutral event or stimulus (the conditioned stimulus or CS) is paired with an unconditioned stimulus (US) which produces an unpleasant emotional state such as fear, it will, after a suitable number of pairings, come to elicit a conditioned response (CR). Surprisingly, this theory was never developed in any detail, and has to be deduced from Watson's writings. Indeed, the interest shown in the model has been mainly for historical reasons, and apart from these, it has had limited influence, partly because early attempts at replication did not meet with success.

The basic model was taken up by Mowrer, who developed it into what has become known as the 'two-process theory' of fear and avoidance (Mowrer 1939, 1940). In contrast to the earlier model, the two-process theory has enjoyed a major influence on psychologists' view of fear since it was formulated. Although the theory has been modified in a number of respects, Mowrer's original idea was that anxiety is best considered as a conditioned pain reaction ' . . . anxiety is a learned response occurring to signals that are premonitory of situations of injury or pain'. (Mowrer 1939, p.565)

Fear and avoidance are established by two processes, the first of which is the classical conditioning of fear to stimuli associated with the painful event. The second process is the reinforcement by fear reduction of any responses which remove the individual from the fear-producing stimuli. This escape behaviour will eventually become avoidance and may lead to well-established behaviour patterns of the type frequently seen in the clinic – for example, the avoidance of footpaths near to grass verges, by Pat, or shops, by Lyn, both mentioned in the Introduction.

Although since its inception the theory has undergone a number of amendments and changes of emphasis (e.g. Miller

1948; Mowrer 1960), it has attracted a number of criticisms which have eventually been too much for it to accommodate. An examination of these criticisms will throw light on the requirements demanded of any comprehensive theory of anxiety, and some of these will be addressed here.

In the first place, established, successful avoidance behaviour appears to be independent of any mediating state of anxiety; whereas for the two-process model to have credence, it is suggested that there would need to be some evidence of fear as a precursor of avoidance. However, if this is measured by autonomic indices of arousal, an obvious fear reaction is not always present prior to successful avoidance. Rescorla and Solomon (1967) concluded, in their review of the research, that no peripheral conditioned responses had been identified as necessary precursors of avoidance, a position later supported by Seligman and Johnston (1973). Carr (1979) also notes from clinical observations that phobic patients are not normally anxious when they are avoiding their phobic stimulus. However, it is necessary to distinguish between causal factors in the original conditioning and subsequent maintaining factors. It is possible that whereas avoidance may have been preceded by discernible autonomic arousal initially, and reinforced by reduction, after a lapse of time it may be maintained by alternative contingencies. It is conceivable that in certain circumstances, for instance, there may be social 'pay-offs' for evincing a fear reaction, such as the attention, sympathy or interest of others.

A second potential problem for the conditioning theory is that in the laboratory, successful conditioning is usually obtained only when the temporal patterning of the CS and the US is very strictly controlled. For example, a gap of between $\frac{1}{2}$ and $2\frac{1}{2}$ seconds from the onset of the CS to the onset of the US is usually considered optimal for, say, eyeblink conditioning to take place. Eysenck (1980) points out that real-life situations are unlikely to be so precisely presented, and that times greatly exceeding the optimal CS/US interval are much more likely. If this is indeed the case, the establishment of a conditioned reaction by the usually accepted process must be questioned. However, by the same token, this may explain why different individuals may undergo similar experiences and only some of them acquire a conditioned avoidance response.

Third, clinical observations on the development of fear do not always accord with the processes specified by the conditioning model. It assumes that all fears are traumatically conditioned, yet clinically it is often difficult to determine the origin of a client's phobia. A study by Rimm *et al.* (1977) reported that only around one-third of the subjects they interviewed could recall an instance of direct conditioning which led to their fears. Murray and Foote (1979), in a study of the origins of fear of snakes, concluded that their results offered very little support for the idea that fear of snakes was acquired on the basis of direct conditioning. Ost and Hugdahl (1981) examined the origins of the fears of phobic clients and reported that just over half of these clients ascribed their phobias to conditioning experiences. Evidence such as this casts grave doubts on the comprehensiveness of the conditioning theory, since many fears do not seem to be traceable to a traumatic event.

Fourth, evidence of fears which have not been acquired through a process of direct conditioning challenges the traditional model yet further. The work of Bandura (1969, 1971) has clearly demonstrated that a good many behavioural and emotional responses may be acquired vicariously, i.e. through observational learning and modelling. The evidence in support of vicarious *acquisition* of fear in humans is indirect and anecdotal, the main direction of Bandura's work being in demonstrating the effective *reduction* of fears by observational learning. Nevertheless, the effectiveness of this method in the reduction of fear does more than simply suggest the possibility that fear may be *acquired* by exposure to fearful models. Furthermore, studies which have directly questioned human subjects on the origins of their fears have recorded that between 6 and 17 per cent of subjects give an account of vicarious learning in the acquisition of their fears (Ost and Hugdahl 1981; Rimm *et al.* 1977).

Fifth, Rachman (1977, 1978b) has documented evidence of failure of human subjects to acquire fears despite exposure to what are, in commonsense terms, extremely fear-provoking situations. He draws on the work of Janis (1951) and Lewis (1942), who report that during Second World War air-raids, when people were exposed to repeated bombing, there was no increase in psychiatric disorders; some short-lived fear reactions were apparently common, but very few phobias developed. The kinds of reactions that people experienced immediately after an air-raid included tremor, fatigue and sleep disturbance, but these usually disappeared after a few days. Such evidence as there is (Janis 1951) suggested that people may even have become more courageous as they were exposed to more numerous and heavy bomb attacks. Rachman argues that observations of such apparent lack of fear in the face of intense trauma and uncertainty run counter to the conditioning theory. According to the theory, large numbers of people should have developed conditioned fear reactions which would have been reinforced with repeated exposures.

Sixth, there has been little convincing demonstration that human fears can be deliberately conditioned under laboratory or clinical settings. Neither English (1929) nor Bregman (1934) were able to replicate Watson and Rayner's original success in conditioning fear, but this may have been because they used inappropriate stimuli – a toy wooden duck or wooden shapes and coloured cloths. Hallam and Rachman (1976), in an evaluation of the status of aversion therapy in alcoholism, noted that electrical aversion did not generate conditioned fear responses as many clinicians appeared to assume. In an attempt to produce a conditioned fear reaction in volunteers using cardiac, skin and respiratory responses to measure this, Hallam and Rachman failed to produce such an effect, even after more than 200 trials with electric shock as the US. Although it has been argued that electric shock is an inappropriate US for producing conditioned aversion to a CS such as taste (Seligman and Hager 1972), the lack of any sign of a conditioned fear response is potentially damaging for a conditioning theory.

Seventh, a further difficulty for the conditioning theory is its assumption, either explicit or implicit, of 'equipotentiality'. This premise assumes that any object or stimulus can acquire the power to evoke a fear response. However, in classical conditioning it is not true to say that any CS and US can be associated equally easily, nor that the laws governing the rate of acquisition and extinction are the same for all CSs and USs (Seligman 1970). An animal experiment by Garcia and Koelling (1966) illustrates the point. Whenever rats drank saccharin-flavoured water, they were exposed to flashing lights and noise. At the same time, they were irradiated, which caused them to be sick an hour later. When tested some time afterwards, it was discovered that the rats had developed a strong aversion to the taste of the water, but not to the noise and lights. The implications of this and other experiments were that some associations between USs and CSs were much more easily made than others.

This led Seligman to invoke the notion of biological 'preparedness' to explain these findings, and he believes that the same notion can be applied to human fears. He has argued:

> A neglected fact about phobias is that, by and large, they comprise a relatively non-arbitrary and limited set of objects: agoraphobia, fear of specific animals, insect phobias, fear of heights and fear of the dark, etc. All these are relatively common phobias. And only very rarely, if ever, do we have pyjama phobias, grass phobias, electric-outlet phobias, hammer phobias, even though these things are likely to be associated with trauma in our world. (Seligman 1971, p.312)

He has gone on to argue that human phobias are of biological significance and that the majority of them are about objects which have threatened the survival of the species, potential predators, unfamiliar places, and the dark. As well as being highly selective, such 'prepared' phobias are held to be very readily acquired, to generalize broadly, and to be highly resistant to extinction.

The frequency with which specific fears occur offers a degree of credibility to the role of preparedness in human fears. A study carried out by Agras, Sylvester and Oliveau (1969) reports findings which favour the notion of preparedness at the expense of the premise of equipotentiality. If all stimuli had an equal chance of becoming conditioned fear stimuli, then a survey of fears in the general population could be expected to show roughly the same prevalence of all fears. The survey by Agras *et al.* has shown clearly that this is not the case. In their 'league table' of common fears, the fear of snakes was most common (390/1,000 population), whereas fear of dentists was only 198/1,000, and fear of injury was 182/1,000. This difference in distribution is despite the fact that contact with dentists was likely to be much more common than contact with snakes, and, like injury, was much more likely to be associated with pain. Against such evidence, the assumption of equipotentiality is not tenable. In spite of this, the preparedness premise has itself drawn some criticism, and its role in the conditioning of fears with evolutionary importance needs to be clarified by further research. For example, Eysenck (1976, p.263) has argued that the concept is circular in that ' . . . it postulates in terms of innate propensities, what requires to be explained'. The hypothesis may be untestable, since it cannot be directly proved or disproved. Despite the final status of the preparedness hypothesis being in some doubt, the non-arbitrary nature of human fears cannot be ignored, and constitutes a further challenge to the conditioning theory.

Eighth, a problem which a conditioning theory has to face is the extreme resistance to extinction shown by some fear responses. Classical conditioning theory states that whenever the CS is presented alone, without being followed by the US, then extinction should take place. A number of theorists have remarked on the apparent failure of extinction to occur and have offered some amendments to the general theory as a result. However, Eysenck (1968, 1976) has argued that in many neuroses, not only does the expected extinction of the CS fail to occur in the absence of further pairings with the

US, but instead there may even be an enhancement effect; this he calls 'incubation'. In such a case, the unreinforced CS actually produces more fear (CR) with each presentation of the CS. Eysenck has drawn heavily on a study by Napalkov (1963) in order to give experimental support to his view. This was a study on dogs involving various USs such as a pistol fired behind a dog's ear to produce as a UR a rise in blood pressure. After 25 repetitions however, the UR habituated to zero. In another group of dogs, the CS was paired with the US on only one occasion. The CS alone was then presented for several hundred trials, and it was discovered that, far from being extinguished, the CR had developed to several times the size of the original UR. The fact that while the UR habituates, the CR augments, is believed by Eysenck to be a classical example of what is meant by enhancement or incubation of the CR. He considers this as very similar to the growth of anxiety to clinical proportions in those who may have undergone a comparatively mild conditioning experience in the first place (Eysenck 1980).

Eysenck has proposed a reformulation of the law of extinction to accommodate this phenomenon, since a Pavlovian account does not allow for a CR ever having greater strength than the UR. In amending the law of extinction, Eysenck (1976) proposes that either extinction or enhancement of the CR might take place. The specific outcome in a given case may depend on a range of factors including the strength of the US and the duration of the CS. A detailed exploration of this theory is beyond the bounds of this volume and interested readers are referred to the original source (Eysenck 1976).

In view of the criticisms that can be levelled against the conditioning model of anxiety, its adequacy as a general theory must be questioned. The limitations of extrapolating from laboratory experiments, frequently with animals, under restricted conditions, must be acknowledged. The relevance of human verbal behaviour to models of anxiety has been afforded far greater emphasis in more recent formulations.

Rachman (1977) has suggested some additional patterns of fear acquisition which need to be incorporated into a comprehensive theory. He proposes that there are three 'pathways' to the acquisition of fear. The first of these is direct conditioning, which he still considers to be an important method of inducing fear and would include fears precipitated by traumatic events. The second proposed pathway is vicarious conditioning, although as mentioned earlier, he accepts that the direct evidence in support of this notion is rather weak. The third pathway which Rachman identifies is by transmission of information and instruction. Again, the evidence in favour of this suggestion is largely anecdotal, but common sense suggests that it is likely that many everyday fears are generated in this way. Rachman concludes that 'any of these three pathways to fear, alone or in combination, can be implicated in the acquisition of fear. By appealing to one or more of these pathways, it should be possible to explain most of the common features of human fear ... ' (Rachman 1977, p.385)

The conditioning model thus amended is undoubtedly the most widely researched theory of fear and anxiety. However, as the following sections show, there has been considerable interest in alternative models of fear acquisition which do not have the conditioning model as their base.

Non-conditioning theories

1. Schachter's 'attribution theory'

Stanley Schachter and his colleagues have proposed a model of emotion which has enjoyed considerable influence. Put simply, Schachter suggests that under certain circumstances, the body experiences a general state of physical arousal characteristic of emotional states. Given such a state of arousal, the individual then labels and interprets the emotion according to factors relating to the current situation and to cognitions stored from previous experiences. It is the latter which determine whether the state of physiological arousal will be labelled 'anger', 'joy', or whatever.

From this position, Schachter has made three general propositions. Firstly, given a state of physiological arousal for which an individual has no explanation, this state will be labelled and the feelings will be described in terms of the cognitions available. Secondly, given a state of physiological arousal for which an individual has a completely appropriate explanation, no evaluative needs will arise, and the individual is unlikely to label these feelings in terms of any alternative cognitions available. Thirdly, given the same cognitive circumstances, the individual will react emotionally or describe feelings as emotions only to the extent that they are experienced as a state of physiological arousal (Schachter 1971).

In an experiment that has since become a classic, Schachter and Singer (1962) attempted to test the hypothesis that the nervous system, in emotion, is in a general state of arousal, but that it is the cognitive labelling or 'attribution' of that arousal which organizes the individual's response. Experimental subjects were told that they would receive an injection of a new vitamin compound to test its effect on vision. In fact, they were injected with either epinephrine (adrenaline) or a 'placebo' injection of saline (in this context a neutral substance). The subjects were divided into four groups: in the first, the 'informed' condition, they were given accurate information on 'side effects' they might experience, and these were the actual effects of epinephrine. In the second, they also were given epinephrine, but were told that there would be no side effects. In the third, the 'misinformed' group, they received epinephrine, but were told to expect side effects which would have been impossible to obtain from epinephrine. In the final condition, the subjects were injected with saline and were told to expect no side effects (the placebo group).

The subjects then encountered another person, a 'stooge', who acted in either an angry or a euphoric manner, and Schachter and Singer's main interest was in the subjects' behaviour with the stooge, as a function of having received epinephrine or not, and whether they had an 'appropriate' explanation for their arousal. Thus, the main interest was in the reactions of the first and third groups. Subjects in the third group, who had been fed the misinformation, showed the greatest tendency to label their emotion in line with that displayed by the stooge, that is either euphoria or anger. Informed subjects, on the other hand, did not tend to produce such labels.

These data suggested that if a state of physiological arousal is induced, and if the individual has no immediate explanation for it, then the state will be labelled in terms of the cognitions available at the time. On the other hand, if the physiological arousal is explicable, in terms of something that has already occurred (e.g. an injection of a given drug), then the individual will have no need to seek an explanation from current environmental events. Further work undertaken around the same time (Schachter and Wheeler 1962) has tended to confirm this view. They showed that subjects demonstrated differential responsiveness to a slapstick comedy film, depending on different cognitions about the source of the arousal.

Subsequent research has shown that an individual's emotionality could be decreased by falsely attributing an emotional state to a non-emotional source. Nisbett and Schachter (1966) demonstrated that subjects who attributed the effects of electric shock to a pill were able to tolerate more shocks than subjects who were not told that the effects were due to a pill.

The implications of research such as this are that the emotions, and more particularly emotional disorders such as anxiety states, may be significantly affected by the attributions that an individual makes about the causes of the various 'symptoms' experienced. A major rôle is thus assigned to the place of cognition in the understanding, and by implication, the treatment of any emotional disorder. However, therapies aimed at persuading people to re-evaluate their interpretation of a perceived emotion, based on the 'mis-attribution' hypothesis, have only modest results to support them. It may enjoy some success when the degree of arousal is relatively small, but its value in countering higher states of arousal is questionable (Mahoney 1974).

2. Lazarus's model

Another formulation of emotion which gives cognition a central role is that proposed by Richard Lazarus and his colleagues. They emphasize the concepts of appraisal and reappraisal as major components of their position. Emotional activity results from the person's appraisal of the situation and whether it is dangerous. It also results from the individual's evaluation of the possibilities for actions that are available to meet the challenge. The terms 'primary' and 'secondary' appraisal have been used to make a distinction between the assessment of the nature of a threat (primary appraisal) and the evaluation of the coping processes available (secondary appraisal). Emotional reactions differ according to the manner in which a threat is appraised; this in turn will affect the coping process. According to their viewpoint: 'The subjective features of emotion derive from the appraised condition of the organism ... Each emotion involves its own particular kind of appraisal, its own particular kinds of action tendencies, and hence its own particular constellation of physiological changes which are part of the mobilisation to action, whether or not these action tendencies are actually expressed or inhibited.' (Lazarus, Averill and Opton 1970, p.218)

In examining the nature of these cognitions (or appraisals) they consider that there are two types of determining conditions: *situational* conditions, which refer to environmental factors, and *dispositional* conditions, which refer to the psychological structure of the individual (e.g. beliefs, attitudes, etc).

The appraisal of a situation includes an evaluation of the outcome, that is, to what extent can the individual cope with the situation and what are the consequences of such coping. They consider also that emotional responses are in a state of being constantly altered: ' ... feedback from the continuous interplay between the conditions causing an emotion and the effects of efforts to cope with them changes the cognitions shaping the emotional reaction'. (Lazarus *et al.* 1970, p.219)

Lazarus has argued that coping processes can be of two kinds. The first consists of *direct action*, with its effect on the environment, which in turn affects the appraisal of the situation. The second type of coping process is cognitive in that it involves further evaluations or reappraisals. As Mandler explains: 'a coping reaction would be a reaction to a particular situation that may be executed and have certain effects as a result of the structures themselves, whereby cognitive or mental restructuring (or reappraisal) may result'. (Mandler 1975, p.107)

This theory and that of Schachter and his colleagues both hold that cognitive processes are indispensable elements of any theory of emotion. They differ in that Lazarus *et al.* believe that each emotion is characterized by its own specific pattern of response, including psychological, behavioural and cognitive components. Schachter, on the other hand, attributes little theoretical importance to physiological differences among emotions, preferring the view that physiological aspects of emotion should be viewed as general activation.

3. Ellis's model

One of the best known descriptions of cognitive processes in emotional disorder and treatment is that described by Albert Ellis (1962) as Rational-Emotive Therapy (RET). Ellis has proposed that people become emotionally disturbed because they develop misperceptions and mistaken cognitions about what they perceive. In addition, emotional under-reaction (or over-reaction) to everyday (or unusual) stimuli contribute to these emotional problems. Ellis has given a summary of his position:

Rational-emotive therapy is based on the assumption that what we label our 'emotional' reactions are caused by our conscious and unconscious evaluations, interpretations and philosophies. Thus, we feel anxious or depressed because we strongly convince ourselves that it is terrible when we fail at something or that we can't stand the pain of being rejected. We feel hostile because we vigorously believe that people who behave unfairly to us absolutely *should not* be the way they indubitably are, and that it is utterly insufferable when they frustrate us. . . . rational-emotive therapy holds that there are virtually no legitimate reasons why human beings need make themselves terribly upset, hysterical or emotionally disturbed, no matter what kind of negative stimuli are impinging on them. (Ellis 1970, quoted by Mahoney 1974, p.170)

From his clinical experience, Ellis has proposed that there are certain core irrational ideas which lie at the base of most emotional disorders. These irrational ideas are:

1. That it is an absolute necessity for an adult to be loved by everyone for everything he or she does – instead of concentrating on building one's self-respect, and on winning approval for practical purposes.
2. That certain acts are awful or wicked, and that people who perform such acts should be severely punished – instead of thinking that certain acts are inappropriate or antisocial, and that people who perform such acts are BEHAVING stupidly.
3. That it is horrible when things are not the way one would like them to be – instead of the idea that it is too bad, that one would better try to change or control conditions so that they become more satisfactory, and, if that is not possible, one had better temporarily accept their existence.
4. That human misery is externally caused and is forced on one by outside people and events – instead of the idea that emotional disturbance is caused by the VIEW one takes of conditions.
5. That if something is or may be dangerous or fearsome one should be terribly upset about it – instead of the idea that one would better frankly face it and render it non-dangerous.

6. That it is easier to avoid than to face life difficulties – instead of thinking that the 'easy' way may in fact prove much harder in the long run.

7. That one needs something other or stronger or greater than oneself on which to rely – instead of the idea that it is better to take the risks of thinking and acting independently.

8. That one should be thoroughly competent, intelligent and achieving in all possible respects – instead of thinking that one should do as well as possible, while accepting that one is not perfect, is human, and therefore makes mistakes.

9. That because something once strongly affected one's life, it should indefinitely affect it – instead of the idea that one can learn from one's past experiences, but should not be totally prejudiced by them.

10. That one must have certain and perfect control over things – instead of the idea that the world is full of probability and chance and that one can still enjoy life despite this.

11. That human happiness can be achieved by inertia and inaction – instead of the idea that humans tend to be happiest when they are vitally absorbed in creative pursuits, or when they are devoting themselves to people or projects outside themselves.

12. That one has virtually no control over one's emotions and that one cannot help feeling certain things – instead of thinking that one has enormous control over one's destructive emotions and that one can choose to work at changing them in more positive directions.

(After Ellis 1970)

Apart from asserting the primacy of these twelve irrational ideas, Ellis has not elaborated a theoretical model from his approach. It is often difficult to distinguish the theory from the practice of RET, and any assumptions underlying the model have to be gleaned from Ellis's clinical writings.

Perhaps the most obvious assumption is that RET holds

that the rationality in thought is all-important, and even equates this rationality with adaptiveness. This view is open to debate, and probably marks out a major distinction between RET and the other cognitive restructuring methods, which tend to emphasize the adaptiveness of thoughts rather than their rationality *per se*.

4. Beck's model

The work of Aaron Beck has added substantially to the notions of dysfunctional thought put forward by Ellis. In Beck's model, cognitions are also ascribed a causal role in determining emotions and behaviour, and emotional disorders are considered to result from cognitive deficits. The major therapeutic implication is that by modifying dysfunctional cognitions, emotional disturbance can be alleviated.

Beck's original work focused on the presence of irrational thoughts in depression, and he used the label the 'cognitive triad' to describe the trilogy of cognitions which he held to be crucial in this disorder (Beck 1976). This cognitive triad consists of negative cognitions about the self, a negative view of the present, and a nihilistic outlook on the future. These negative cognitions are also called 'automatic thoughts', because they seem to occur almost automatically, and extremely rapidly. He has described their characteristics (1976, pp.36–7) as follows:

1. They [automatic thoughts] generally are not vague and unformulated, but are specific and *discrete*. They occur in a kind of shorthand; that is, only the essential words in a sentence seem to occur – as in telegraphic style.
2. The thoughts do not arise as a result of deliberation, reasoning or reflection about an event or topic. There is no logical sequence of steps such as in goal-oriented thinking, or problem-solving. The thoughts 'just happen' ... They just seem to be relatively *autonomous* in that the patient made no effort to initiate them and in more disturbed cases they are difficult to 'turn off'.
3. The patient tends to regard these automatic thoughts as

> *plausible* or reasonable, although they may seem far-
> fetched to somebody else ... The content of automatic
> thoughts, particularly those that are repetitive and seem to
> be most powerful, are idiosyncratic.

A second main element of Beck's model is the postulated existence of cognitive structures or schemata. These schemata are maladaptive beliefs or 'silent assumptions' which constitute the sets of rules which individuals use to structure their experiences. These maladaptive beliefs are held to be idiosyncratic (unlike Ellis's 'irrational beliefs'), and probably are established in childhood, and may be activated under certain stressful circumstances in later life.

A third important component of Beck's model lies in his outline of some broad categories of dysfunctional thought which are evident in emotional disorders. Beck specifies six overlapping types of thinking error. *Arbitrary inference* refers to the drawing of a conclusion when evidence is lacking or is actually contrary to the conclusion. *Over-generalization* refers to the drawing of a general conclusion on the basis of a single incident. *Magnification* (or minimization) refers to the tendency to exaggerate the importance of a negative event (or to undervalue the importance of a positive event). *Cognitive deficiency* involves disregarding an important aspect of a life situation, with a tendency to fail to integrate or to utilize relevant information derived from experience. *Personalization* refers to a tendency to relate external events to the self when there is no basis for making such a connection. Finally, *dichotomous thinking*, noted by Lazarus (1971), refers to the tendency to think or evaluate events in extreme terms with no attention being paid to any 'middle ground'.

Beck holds that the key difference between different types of emotional disorder is the content of the cognitions. For each of the neurotic disorders, Beck has suggested specific ideational contents, as listed in Table 4.1 (after Mahoney and Arnkoff 1978, p.706). In his attempt to construct a model of anxiety, Beck suggests that some precipitating event or

Table 4.1 Ideational content of the emotional disorders

Disorder	Cognitive content
1. Depression	1. Thoughts centring on the experience of loss along with (a) devaluation of self (b) a negative view of life experiences (c) a pessimistic view of the future
2. Anxiety	2. Thoughts of danger predominate
3. Paranoia	3. Thoughts focus on interference and intrusion by other people
4. Obsession	4. Thoughts generally focus on doubts (e.g. about a past performance or a future capacity)

events elicit some underlying attitude of fear, and that this activates a series of ideas related to danger. The individual then becomes primed to seek out further 'dangerous' elements in the environment. It is suggested that when new situations which might have unpleasant outcomes are encountered, they are construed as dangerous. The model is developed further:

> Danger-related ideation is subsequently more easily activated by less specific, less avoidable, more internal classes of stimuli. Even more subtle aspects of relatively non-threatening situations begin to be associated with such cognitions. Such ideation is accompanied by experiences and bodily sensations of anxiety, which reinforce the underlying attitude. As the situations become less avoidable, more frequent, and unpredictable, the patient becomes more apprehensive about losing control of his anxiety. Perhaps his 'stream of consciousness' regularly contains more danger-related ideation with only slight or no relevance to environmental events. Prolonged activation of such ideation results in anxiety neurosis.
>
> Although stimulus situations may initially be rather analogous to the precipitating events, after repeated hypervigilance they become less clearly related to the precipitating events ... An increasingly fixed cognitive organisation ensues so that once a

situation is labelled as 'dangerous' by the patient, the association is left unquestioned; his thinking is dominated by the concept of danger. The patients fix on specific possibilities of situations and anticipate 'danger' with which they believe they cannot cope. Other less dangerous possibilities are apparently discounted or not experienced at all. The likelihood of danger is felt as high. (Beck and Rush 1975, pp.76–7).

In summary, the characteristics of the dysfunctional thoughts of anxiety are that they repetitively construe harmful or dangerous events, that they cannot be 'reasoned away' and that they become readily attached to a wide range of stimuli which can evoke them.

Experimental background of the models

A notable difference between the 'conditioning' and the 'non-conditioning' theories of fear acquisition lies in the degree to which they have been investigated experimentally. A considerable body of literature has been spawned by interest in one form or another of the conditioning model. A large part of this literature has come from experiments with animals, since many aspects of the conditioning model lend themselves to testing on non-human subjects. By contrast, the experimental data generated by most of the non-conditioning theories are rather thin. The fact that the non-conditioning theories cannot be evaluated by using non-human subjects does not in itself account for the difference.

An important distinction between the two types of theory may be that a number of the non-conditioning models have been formulated primarily by clinicians rather than experimentalists or theoreticians. As a consequence, the 'theory' and the 'practice' derived from non-conditioning models are perhaps much more closely linked than they are in the conditioning model. The emphasis has been on generating effective clinical interventions rather than answering theoretical questions which may have been posed for their own sake. The resulting experimental data have tended to emphasize clinical features rather than refine some theoretical issue which may or may not have any direct clinical bearing. This leaves them open to the criticism that, although they have produced laudably detailed descriptions of the phenomena of anxiety-related cognitions, they have failed, as yet, to provide an adequate account of their genesis and development. It must be concluded that the models of anxiety emphasizing cognitive events are at a much earlier stage of theoretical development.

A comprehensive theory of anxiety must address a number of issues. It must, for example, deal adequately with the means by which anxiety is generated. Rachman (1977) has already attempted to identify the 'pathways to fear' and considers that three such pathways exist. These have been mentioned earlier in the chapter and include direct conditioning, vicarious conditioning and direct instruction. A theory must also deal with the diverse symptoms that can present as anxiety. In particular, the theory has to accommodate the three classes of symptoms (somatic, cognitive and behavioural) and account for the lack of correlation among these three systems. This is far from straightforward, as Hugdahl (1981) has pointed out. The primacy of these systems is disputed by various schools of thought, and the indication of a causal link from one system to another would be a major achievement for any theoretical formulation of anxiety.

It may be, however, that we should not look exclusively to the ways in which anxiety is *generated* in order to explain why some people develop incapacitating fears. After all, it is quite likely that many people are exposed to very frightening circumstances and yet no phobic anxiety develops. As we have seen, Rachman (1977) has drawn attention to the work of Janis (1951) and Lewis (1942) who studied people who had been exposed to repeated bombing during air-raids in the Second World War. Despite this exposure to frequent air-raids, very few phobias were reported. Rather than concentrating on the direct conditioning of fears, it may be worth while examining the factors governing the *extinction* of conditioned emotional responses. In other words, we may all be subject to traumatic conditioning events, and the likelihood that only a relatively small number of people go on to develop phobias may have more to do with their inability to show rapid extinction. Any theory of anxiety must take this into account. There may, for example, be clinical implications for understanding whether a fear or anxiety exists: (a) because of the method by which it was generated, or (b) because of its failure to extinguish. There has been some speculation on these issues, but as yet there is little empirical support for the various theoretical considerations mentioned here.

Chapter 5

The treatment of anxiety: behavioural methods

Over the years a number of strategies have evolved for the management of anxiety by psychological means. Many of these methods have focused on specific fears or phobias, and more recently there has been a move to look at ways of helping people with more generalized forms of anxiety. There is a considerable variability in the degree to which these therapeutic methods have been experimentally validated. The aim here is to give a description of the clinical method and its application, followed by some discussion of the evidence for its effectiveness. This chapter focuses on the earlier treatment methods which have sprung primarily from the experimental behavioural literature, and Chapter 6 looks at the more recent development of therapies which have their base within the cognitive school.

Relaxation

Very many of the methods used to treat anxiety problems teach the client to use a systematic method of relaxation. The rationale behind this is that it is impossible for the body to be physically relaxed and tense at the same time. Numerous methods have been used to teach people to relax. As many as 25 different methods have been distinguished in the available literature. However, four main methods can be discerned which are in current clinical use, most of the others being variations of these.

One of the most widely used methods is known as *progressive muscle relaxation* or *Jacobsonian relaxation*, after the physician who originally described the method. The subject is normally lying down or seated in a comfortable chair, and is asked deliberately to tense up a group of muscles, say those in the hands. The fists are clenched as tightly as possible, and after a few seconds gently relaxed while the client is instructed to focus on the difference between the feelings of tension and relaxation. A second muscle group may then be selected, say the muscles of the lower arm, and the tension/relaxation sequence is repeated. All of the muscle groups of the body are worked through in this manner, usually in some systematic order, such as from head to toe. The aims of this method are both to achieve a state of muscular relaxation, and also to teach the subject to discriminate the difference between tension and relaxation. This is to encourage the development of a greater degree of voluntary control over the physical state of tension in the future. During the learning stages, the exercise may be performed under the guidance of a trained therapist, but it is now a frequent practice to provide the client with tape-recorded instructions so that practice may be more readily carried out at home. In its original form, described by Jacobson (1938), training took up to 60 hours, but at the present 10 or 12 half-hour sessions are more usual.

In contrast to Jacobson's method, *autogenic relaxation training* (Schultz and Luthe 1959) does not require the prior induction of a state of tension before relaxing. In this method, the subject is asked to focus on a part of the body, say the arm, and to concentrate on producing feelings of warmth and relaxation in that limb. Gradually the other limbs and muscle systems may be asked to imagine they have control over various organs in the body, not normally under their voluntary control. Once relaxation of the musculature has been achieved, the person may be instructed to concentrate on producing relaxing mental images.

Various procedures from the world of *meditation* have

also been used in clinics to induce relaxation. One example of these is that of Benson (1975). The method incorporates four elements deemed to be present in most of the meditational systems. These are as follows:

1. A quiet environment, with as few distractions. as possible.
2. A mental device. In order to prevent intrusive thoughts, subjects are asked to focus their attention on the act of breathing, and also to repeat quietly to themselves a word or phrase with each outward breath.
3. A passive attitude. Subjects are instructed that intrusive thoughts will occur from time to time, but these should be disregarded and attention should be focused again on the repeated word. Subjects are told not to be tempted to force themselves to relax, but simply to practise the breathing exercise, repeat the chosen word and let any relaxation happen of its own accord.
4. A comfortable position. Many meditation procedures involve a particular posture to be adopted during practice, which may have evolved to prevent falling asleep. For this reason a sitting position is preferred to lying down when practising relaxation.

The subject is instructed to close the eyes and concentrate on nothing other than the intake and exhalation of each breath. After a short time the person is asked to introduce the relaxing word (or *mantra*) to be repeated inwardly with each outward breath. These words should be individually chosen by each subject, but words such as 'relax' or 'calm' are often picked. The whole procedure normally takes around 15 minutes, and is practised several times daily. After the skill has been developed, subjects can often induce a deep level of relaxation after only several minutes.

Another system of relaxation training has utilized *bio-feedback*. Put simply, a key physiological response is monitored using specialized equipment and its reactivity is displayed to the person either visually or auditorily. For example, this may be direct feedback from muscles, heart rate or electrodermal activity. It has been demonstrated that this extra feedback helps the individual gain control over a physiological system which would otherwise be outside voluntary control. Electrodes are placed on the surface of the skin to monitor the response. The subject may either hear a click which varies in frequency or observe a needle move across a dial according to the activity of the system. As with other methods of relaxation, biofeedback requires considerable practice before subjects can influence reliably the system being monitored. A subject undergoing biofeedback training can be seen in Fig. 3.1.

The equipment used can be highly sophisticated and is therefore based in clinics, but smaller, portable units may be made available for home use. Despite initial enthusiasm for this method, it has proved rather disappointing (Carroll 1984). Although the activity of physiological systems can be influenced, this is rarely to such an extent as to be of clinical significance. Further difficulties lie in trying to have the subject generalize any response which is achieved outside the clinical setting, i.e. when away from the apparatus.

Whichever method of relaxation induction is used, it is important to stress to clients that they are engaged in developing a skill. Like any other skill this requires practice before it can be properly used to deal with high degrees of anxiety or tension.

Systematic desensitization

Among the earliest of the behavioural treatments of anxiety was systematic desensitization. Although the basic idea behind the method had been appreciated by a number of writers (e.g. Herzberg 1941; Jones 1924), credit is generally given to Joseph Wolpe as the main pioneer (Wolpe 1954, 1958). Wolpe considered that the mechanism of desensitization was based on the principle of reciprocal inhibition, which could be stated in the following way: 'If a response antagonistic to anxiety can be made to occur in the presence of anxiety-evoking stimuli so that it is accompanied by a complete or partial suppression of the anxiety responses, the bond between these stimuli and the anxiety responses will be weakened.' (Wolpe 1958, p.71)

Several response patterns were considered to be incompatible with anxiety, including sexual arousal and respiratory responses, but by far the most widely used response has been deep muscle relaxation, based on Jacobson's (1938) method and described earlier. Systematic desensitization is a method that has been most frequently used in cases where the anxiety experienced is related to *specific* situations or objects. The procedure comprises three stages. In the first place, the individual is instructed in relaxation exercises. An initial prerequisite of systematic desensitization, as described by Wolpe, was that no further progress could be attained until the person was able to reach a deeply relaxed state at will. More recent research has questioned this, and we will return to this point later in the chapter.

The second stage is to develop a hierarchy of anxiety-producing stimuli. The purpose of this is to rank-order objects or elements of a situation according to subjective ratings of anxiety associated with each. It is useful to ask the subject to assign a figure between 0 and 100, indicating the degree of anxiety. This has been referred to as a 'subjective units of discomfort scale' (SUDS) (Wolpe and Lazarus 1966). Establishing a reliable hierarchy requires considerable clinical skill. The clinician must ensure that all key features are included and this may necessitate detailed probing at interview. The client may not initially be able to break down the aspects of the phobic stimulus into the elements required, and may need considerable help to do so. Typical problems are an inability to produce items in the middle range of the hierarchy. A hierarchy, if it is to be effective, should be thought of as a ladder with evenly spaced rungs. A ladder with a few rungs at the bottom and then no more until near the top would be of little use. Other difficulties sometimes encountered are unstable ratings of items (i.e. the amount of fear with respect to an item may fluctuate, thus changing its position in the hierarchy) and anticipated ratings do not always match the amount of fear generated by the actual presentation of the item.

The third stage, having taught the skills of relaxation and having established the hierarchy, has been known as counter-conditioning. The individual, while in a state of deep relaxation, is presented with the first item on the hierarchy. If the hierarchy has been properly drawn up, the amount of fear usually associated with this item should be readily controlled by the relaxation which has been induced. The next item on the hierarchy should not be introduced until the subject feels entirely comfortable in the presence of the first item. The principle underlying systematic desensitization is that subjects should not experience anxiety at any point in their progress up the hierarchy.

The method will be more clearly demonstrated by an example. Pat, whose phobia of worms was described in the Introduction, produced the hierarchy in Table 5.1.

Desensitization may occur most effectively when it is conducted *in vivo* i.e. with exposure to real-life situations (Sherman 1972), although imaginal desensitization has also proved effective in many cases (Paul 1969). In this case the client is instructed to imagine the various scenes, or objects

Table 5.1 Hierarchy for a worm/maggot phobia

SUDs	
10	Maggot in sealed jar 6 ft away
20	Maggot 3 ft away – no lid on jar
30	Maggot in gloved hand
40	Worm in sealed jar 6 ft away
50	Holding sealed jar containing small worm
60	Live worm held 3 ft away by therapist
70	Dead worm held 1 ft away by therapist
80	Live worm held 1 ft away by therapist
90	Holding dead worm in gloved hand
100	Holding live worm in gloved hand

which figure in the hierarchy. Sometimes a mixture of imagination and *in vivo* exposure may be used, especially when the phobia is of something which is inaccessible to *in vivo* exposure, such as flashes of lightning.

During the 1960s and 1970s, desensitization became one of the most widely researched psychological treatment methods, and its effectiveness was put beyond doubt. Paul's (1969) review of all available controlled studies of desensitization, covering almost 1,000 different clients treated by over 90 different therapists, led him to conclude ' . . . for the first time in the history of psychological treatments, a specific therapeutic package reliably produced measurable benefits for clients across a broad range of distressing problems in which anxiety was of fundamental importance'. (Paul 1969, p.159)

There is no doubt that systematic desensitization is an effective procedure. There have, however, been debates about the most effective form (Rimm and Masters 1979) and about the appropriateness of some of the experimental populations which have been studied (Bernstein and Paul 1971; Borkovec and Rachman 1979). In addition to establishing the effectiveness of desensitization, attention has also been paid to the mechanisms by which it achieves its effects. Wolpe's original notion that reciprocal inhibition was the key factor in operation has been substantially discredited. A number of experimental studies have questioned the necessity of some of the basic procedural requirements, such as the need for an individually tailored hierarchy (Krapf and Nawas 1970), and the need for a deep state of relaxation to be induced prior to hierarchy presentation (Sue 1972). Furthermore, the effectiveness of an alternative treatment – flooding, which will be discussed in the next section – poses a challenge to the notions underlying systematic desensitization.

The indications are that exposure to the fear-producing object or situation is the crucial factor in successful desensitization (Davison and Wilson 1973; Wilson and Davison 1971). However, besides exposure, desensitization probably involves such things as cognitive relabelling, client expectancy and social reinforcement; a review by Kazdin and Wilcoxon (1976) addresses in some detail the methodological issues involved in the evaluation of treatment effects. Although Yates (1975) anticipated that desensitization would meet its imminent demise, it continues to enjoy popularity as a clinical method of fear reduction (Marshall 1981).

Flooding

Whereas desensitization involves a gradual exposure to the feared object or situation, flooding is a much more rapid procedure. Its aim is to confront the feared object as quickly as possible. When the feared object is introduced, the person is required to remain in its presence for a considerable length of time. As prolonged exposure to the object/situation is a crucial element of the treatment, it is important to prevent the individual from escaping or avoiding the situation. In practice this will mean that the individual will not only remain in physical proximity to the object, but must also be encouraged to maintain attention to it.

The theory behind flooding is that the avoidance behaviour is normally reinforced by a reduction in anxiety. If the avoidance behaviour is prevented, then anxiety will occur. The duration of exposure is dependent on the individual's response in the clinical situation and it is important to maintain the person in the situation until the anxiety dissipates. This might be monitored by self-report (e.g. subjective units of distress) or by some physiological monitoring device. Therefore, the treatment period may take a variable amount of time, usually several hours, but perhaps as long as a day. It is, therefore, important for the clinician to make available an appropriate amount of time.

In so far as flooding involves prolonged exposure to anxiety-provoking stimuli, it seems at face value to be almost the opposite of desensitization. Indeed, Wolpe (1969) went as far as to warn that ' ... exposure, and prolonged exposure in particular can seriously enhance phobic sensitivity'. (Wolpe 1969, p.127) Although a review by Morganstern (1973) concluded that there was no convincing evidence that flooding was effective in humans, a number of other studies have noted its efficacy (Gelder *et al.* 1973; Marks, Boulougouris and Marset 1971; Marshall, Gauthier and Gordon 1979). Considerable interest had been given to the relative merits of flooding versus desensitization. The study by Marks *et al.* (1971) found some advantage for flooding over desensitization, but Gelder and his colleagues (1973) as well as Marshall *et al.* (1979) found no significant difference between the two methods. Marks (1975), on the other hand, reviewed evidence suggesting the superiority of flooding with agoraphobics.

It is likely that much of the conflicting evidence on flooding has been due to procedural variations in executing the technique. Such factors as the number of sessions, the duration of exposure, whether it is *in vivo* or in fantasy, whether it is carried out in a group and whether therapist modelling is involved, are all considerations which may influence the outcome (Marks 1978b).

If there is little, if any, difference between the outcome of flooding and desensitization, it may be asked why one method should be chosen for an intervention rather than the other. There is a lack of guidance on this topic in the literature, and such advice as there is would seem to be based on largely anecdotal evidence. Marshall (1981), for example, suggests that such client characteristics as the particular nature of the fear, willingness to tolerate anxiety and the urgency of the need for behaviour change will influence the choice of method. In addition, he notes that therapist factors, such as being bored by administering desensitization or being too distressed themselves by carrying out flooding, may contribute to the choice. Lazarus and Wilson (1976) advise that it is important to establish that the client can safely experience any discomfort entailed in flooding. A further factor is the relative speed which either method takes to administer, and this must favour flooding, which usually takes less time (Marshall 1981).

However, at a practical level, there are certain clinical problems which may preclude the use of flooding for practical or 'risk' considerations, e.g. if someone has a specific fear of driving, it might not be advisable to immediately expose them to the most feared aspect, possibly driving fast on a motorway. If strong anxiety arose, then considerable danger may occur to the subject as well as to other road users. Flooding may also be inappropriate when the occurrence of the object or situation is beyond human control. It is difficult, for example, to flood someone with a fear of thunder, since the phobic event cannot be presented in a controlled manner. It should be added that flooding should not be undertaken by an individual who is not accompanied by a therapist. Although it may be appropriate for clients to undertake unsupervised sessions of desensitization, they should never attempt flooding without expert guidance.

Flooding is also used in the treatment of obsessive-compulsive problems, and when it is, it is usually accompanied by a procedure called response prevention. Among the early reports of the use of response prevention is that of Levy and Meyer (1971). The term refers to the active prevention of ritualistic behaviour, usually following exposure to those stimuli which normally elicit it. For example, a subject might feel compelled to wash repeatedly after briefly touching a carpet. If a response prevention procedure was being operated, the subject would be required to touch the carpet, but then be prevented from washing. After touching the carpet, it is likely that intense feelings of anxiety would be experienced, and the compulsion to wash would be very strong. Initially, the subject would be closely supervised by a therapist, and any attempt to wash would be discouraged, and physically prevented if necessary. Gradually the anxiety would diminish, and as a result the compulsion to wash would become less strong. When the anxiety eventually subsides, the procedure would be repeated until no, or very little, anxiety were experienced following 'contamination'.

The degree of supervision required for this procedure will vary according to the stage of treatment, and also from subject to subject. At the beginning of treatment, continual supervision may be necessary to ensure that the ritual is controlled. After a few days or possibly a few hours depending on the subject, the supervision can be relaxed as the subject becomes better able to control the ritual.

Rachman, Hodgson and Marks, in a series of studies (Rachman, Hodgson and Marks 1971; Rachman, Marks and Hodgson 1973; Marks, Hodgson and Rachman 1975), have demonstrated the effectiveness of flooding and response prevention with obsessional subjects. It is now probably the treatment of choice for this type of problem, and it has been known to produce improvement in people with chronic and severe obsessions.

Modelling

Although modelling may be an important component of both desensitization and flooding, it is worth some consideration in its own right. The method owes much to Albert Bandura and his colleagues who both developed and refined it (Bandura 1969, 1971; Bandura, Grusec and Menlove 1967; Bandura and Menlove 1968).

Modelling techniques seek to reduce fearful behaviour by having the client observe one or more people who perform effectively in the situation which the client fears. Rimm and Masters (1979) have noted that modelling may serve four basic functions: it may serve to teach the observer new behaviour patterns, thus serving an *acquisition* function. It may provide social *facilitation* of appropriate behaviours, by inducing clients to perform behaviours which they are already able to do, but which are not being used to best advantage. Thirdly, modelling may lead to the *disinhibition* of behaviour that has been previously avoided because of fear and anxiety. Related to this, but listed separately, modelling may promote the *vicarious and direct extinction* of the fear associated with the object or situations involved. As far as the use of modelling in the treatment of anxiety is concerned, it is the third and fourth of Rimm and Master's functions that are of most interest.

There is a good deal of evidence that modelling effectively modifies fear-related behaviour (Bandura, Blanchard and Ritter 1969; Bandura, Jeffery and Gajdos 1975; Bandura, Jeffery and Wright 1974), although the bulk of research has been done on non-clinical populations. A number of variables have been found to have a bearing on the effectiveness of modelling. For example, when clients are invited to participate in the behaviour which the model has demonstrated, the effectiveness of the procedure is substantially enhanced (Bandura, Blanchard and Ritter 1969; Blanchard 1970). For example, Ritter (1968) used vicarious and participant modelling techniques in a group desensitization procedure for children with snake phobias. Some of the children watched the experimenter and peer models engage in gradually bolder interactions with a tame 4 ft Gopher snake, while others not only observed but also had opportunity to make physical contact with the model-therapists and the snake. Treatment effectiveness was measured by a behavioural avoidance test and results showed that 80 per cent of the participant group and 53 per cent of the vicarious group completed the terminal task of the avoidance test which was to sit with the snake in their lap for 30 seconds. None of the members of the treatment control group was able to do this.

A number of other factors have been found to enhance the power of the model in influencing behaviour change. Live models may be preferable to symbolic models such as use of video or audio-taped recordings of models encountering feared situations or the use of written scripts. With live models the observer may be said to become more attentive to the procedure which portrays a real human being coping with a 'here and now' situation. However, the use of symbolic models may confer certain practical advantages to the clinician such as ease of access and the greater degree of control that can be exerted to edit the material to avoid unplanned occurrences or inappropriately modelled behaviour. Perceived competence and high status have also been found to be characteristics which enhance the power of the model, although this is within certain limits. If the model is too advanced in his or her display of coping, there is a danger of the subject dismissing what may be seen as an unrealistic goal. Perceived similarity of model to subject is also an important factor and so ideally the model should display behavioural competence just one or two steps ahead of the student. Possibly the use of an 'old boy' may have a part to play, that is, someone who has experienced the same difficulties in the past but who has overcome them sufficiently to model coping skills for others less advanced in treatment. This method would utilize a number of criteria demonstrated to be effective, namely a live model, with perceived similarity to the student, who verbalizes initial uncertainty but subsequently demonstrates successful coping strategies to reach the goal behaviour. Finally, it is important to use a variety of models differing in ages, sex and socio-economic status in a range of related situations to aid generalization.

A real-life example might help to illustrate how some of these factors can work in practice. Let us take the case of Brenda, whose obsessional problems were described at the end of Chapter 2. Brenda was seen initially as an outpatient, but it soon became clear that she would need more intensive treatment if she was to begin to make any improvement. She was then admitted to hospital, and an intensive exposure and modelling programme was begun. On the ward, Brenda watched while her therapist deliberately 'contaminated' himself by rubbing a soiled tea-towel over his arms, legs, body, and eventually over his face. She visibly cringed as she watched this display, and had to be encouraged to keep watching. After the therapist had finished, other members of staff stepped forward, so that they in turn could be 'contaminated' by the same tea-towel. A number of people had volunteered for this task, including student nurses, the ward sister, an orderly and several doctors. As Brenda continued to watch, she became less anxious as she saw that the volunteers did not experience any fear, and took the contamination in their stride. Eventually she was persuaded to touch the cloth and put it over her own clothes. This made her extremely fearful for a short while, but the fear gradually died down. Similar tactics were taken with a wide range of items, and while in hospital, Brenda could cope without having to wash herself thoroughly afterwards.

The next step was to take the treatment into Brenda's home environment, to try to ensure that generalization would occur after she left the hospital. The same team of therapists went with Brenda to her home. Once there, they began to 'contaminate' themselves with items which Brenda could not bring herself to touch, or could only do so if she was able to introduce her washing rituals to cleanse herself. The items used in this contamination included towels, the contents of a laundry bucket, a duster and some waste paper. After watching the therapists while they handled these items, Brenda attempted to do the same, initially with great trepidation, but much more readily after a short while. On subsequent visits, the team was joined by a range of Brenda's friends, who agreed to participate in the programme in order to provide as wide range of models as possible. The treatment continued until Brenda was able to cope with the normal chores she would need to carry out in her flat, to which she successfully returned following treatment.

The models in this example illustrated a number of points. Firstly, some were of high status (the therapists and medical staff). Secondly, they demonstrated *competence*. Thirdly, the modelling was *live* (rather than, for example, on film or videotape). Fourthly, some of the models were *similar* in age and background to the client (her friends). Finally, a wide *variety* of models were employed. These various factors are among those considered to be the effective components of a modelling programme.

Chapter 6

The treatment of anxiety: cognitive and group methods

While the traditional approaches described in the previous chapter have enjoyed a good deal of success and popularity, clinicians are currently showing a great deal of interest in cognitive therapy. This type of treatment is warmly welcomed by many, but its introduction into the behavioural camp has met with many pockets of resistance. It may appear to be too mentalistic for those from hard-line behavioural backgrounds, but empirical demonstrations of its effectiveness will have to be acknowledged. Many questions about its effectiveness remain, as yet, unanswered, but despite this it has undoubted clinical appeal. Several 'brands' of cognitive therapy can be broadly distinguished, although there is often an apparent overlap among them.

Rational-emotive therapy

One of the earliest acknowledged cognitive therapies and one which has received a great deal of attention has been Albert Ellis's Rational-Emotive Therapy (RET). As already mentioned in Chapter 4, RET holds that emotional disorders are caused by maladaptive thoughts and beliefs. At the root of most disorders there are said to be a number of core irrational ideas or assumptions which are considered to be responsible for an individual's distress.

The method of conducting RET is closely tied to the

theoretical assumptions which it holds. The essence of RET can be symbolized as an *A-B-C-D-E* paradigm (Ellis 1971). *A* refers to some real-life event to which an individual is exposed. *B* refers to the chain of thoughts of self-statements which follow that event. *C* is taken to symbolize the negative emotions and behaviours that are a consequence of B. *D* represents the therapist's attempts to modify the future occurrence of the responses which take place at *B*. *E* is the beneficial effects in terms of emotion and behaviour which, hopefully, follow the therapist's intervention.

The therapist can be said to have three main tasks. In the first place, the external events which precipitate episodes of anxiety, have to be determined. Secondly, considerable attention is paid to the specific thought patterns and underlying beliefs that the individual experiences in reaction to the precipitating events. This stage is most important since these thoughts are considered crucial in giving rise to negative emotions. It is also important to train the individual to identify these thoughts, since they can only stand a chance of being changed if they are recognized in the first place. Finally, the client is trained to substitute more rational thoughts in place of the maladaptive beliefs.

Mahoney and Arnkoff (1978) offer a component analysis of RET, and suggest that the clinical approach often includes the following (p.704):

1. Direct instruction and persuasion towards the basic RET premise (i.e. that irrational thoughts play an important role in subjective distress).
2. Recommendations to monitor one's thought patterns.
3. Modelling of a rationalistic evaluation and modification of personal thought patterns.
4. Candid feedback (positive and negative) on reported changes in thinking patterns and self evaluation.
5. Performance assignments and rehearsal tasks to improve discrimination and evaluation of performance-relevant cognitions.

Despite the widespread interest in Rational-Emotive Therapy, there has been a comparative lack of controlled experimental evidence on its effectiveness. Ellis has offered a number of case studies attesting to its efficacy, as have some other clinicians (e.g. Goodman and Maultsby 1974; Watts, Powell and Austin 1973). In addition, there have been several attempts to evaluate the approach more formally, and some of these have produced encouraging results (e.g. Di Loreto 1971; Goldfried, Decenteceo and Weinberg 1974). However, detailed outcome studies on RET have been sparse, and although cognitions have an important part to play in the treatment of anxiety, their precise role needs more clarification. A good deal of the research which has taken place has not specifically focused on RET, but has tended to encompass the wider field of cognitive therapy in general.

Beck's cognitive therapy

The approach taken by Beck has some similarities with RET, and both are examples of what have become known as cognitive restructuring methods. Beck's approach (like Ellis's) often makes it difficult to distinguish theory from therapy, since the latter is the direct practice of the former. Beck attempts to make clients aware of their dysfunctional thought patterns. The form which these may take has already been described in Chapter 4. (As a reminder, these include arbitrary inference, overgeneralization, magnification, selective attention, personalization and dichotomous thinking.) These processes are said to result directly in emotional problems, and the initial steps in Beck's therapy are directed towards having the clients identify the distortions in their thinking styles. Clients are also taught Beck's model, and are encouraged to seek the links between their distorted thinking processes and their emotional states.

The next stage of treatment is to have the clients alter their maladaptive thought processes in favour of more appropriate, constructive patterns. Beck believes that there are a number of stages which any therapeutic intervention involves. He argues:

Since making the incorrect judgements has probably become a
deeply ingrained habit, which he [the client] may not be
conscious of, several steps are required to correct it. First, he
has to become aware of what he is thinking. Second, he needs
to recognize what thoughts are awry. Then he has to
substitute accurate for inaccurate judgements. Finally, he
needs feedback to inform him whether his changes are correct.
The same kind of sequence is necessary for making
behavioural changes, such as improving form in a sport,
correcting faults in playing an instrument, or perfecting
techniques of persuasion. (Beck 1976, p.217)

As well as focusing on cognitions, Beck encourages his
clients to engage in graded behavioural assignments, indulge
in homework tasks and keep activity records. These tasks
may be reviewed during interviews to cast more light on
cognitive distortions and help generate alternative strategies
or interpretations.

Much of the evaluation of Beck's therapy has been carried
out on depressed clients rather than on anxious ones. Beck
(1976) reviewed a number of studies comparing cognitive
therapy and behaviour therapy and combinations of the two
in the treatment of depression. He was able to conclude that
such outcome studies demonstrated the effectiveness of
cognitive therapy. However, most of the studies which he
reviewed have used a student population rather than a
psychiatric one. More recent studies on moderately to
severely depressed clinical populations (for example Rush
and Watkins 1981; Blackburn *et al* 1981) have demonstrated
that cognitive therapy can be effective. There is, as yet, less
convincing evidence of its effectiveness in a clinically anxious
population, but it must be regarded as having considerable
promise.

Self-instruction training

Self-instruction training was popularized by the French
psychotherapist Emile Coué (1922). He is perhaps best
known for coining the statement, 'Day by day, in every way,

I am getting better and better.' However, Donald Meichenbaum and his colleagues are more usually associated with the movement which has concerned itself with those things that clients say to themselves (Meichenbaum 1977; Meichenbaum and Cameron 1974).

Developing his ideas from the work of Luria (1961) and Vygotsky (1962) Meichenbaum became interested in the private speech of impulsive children. In a series of laboratory experiments, he and his colleagues were able to demonstrate that these children could be taught to use self-instruction to slow their reactions and improve their accuracy in performing tasks. Quite literally, the children were taught to talk to themselves about what they were doing. They were told to 'talk themselves through' the tasks they had to do, and by doing so they carried out these tasks much more effectively.

In transferring the technique to adults with emotional problems, there is the implicit assumption that these individuals' cognitions are instances of images and self-statements that do not accurately reflect reality. Given this assumption, one of the first tasks in any therapeutic intervention is to make the client aware of the controlling role of these cognitions in behaviour: clients are asked to examine explicitly the self-statements they make in the situation which causes them to feel anxious. Having identified these statements and recognized their importance in maintaining anxiety, clients are taught to develop more adaptive and realistic statements.

Meichenbaum's work on self-instruction became the platform from which he launched his coping-skills package, 'stress inoculation training'. Various other coping-skills packages had already been described (Goldfried 1971; Suinn and Richardson 1971) and had produced promising results, but stress inoculation has appeared to be arguably a more comprehensive approach within a coherent framework. Mahoney (1974) has characterized the method as involving: (a) a discussion of stress reactions, with emphasis on labelling, attribution, and arousal-inducing self-statements;

(b) relaxation training, presented as an active coping skill; (c) instructed practice in the use of coping self-statements; and (d) supervised practice in using such coping skills, perhaps under real stress-provoking conditions.

A full and detailed account of stress inoculation is provided by Meichenbaum (1977), who has also tried to delineate the treatment components which underlie the different coping skills packages. He believes it is possible to discriminate the following components:

1. Teaching the client the role of cognitions in contributing to the presenting problem through both didactic presentation and guided self-discovery.
2. Training in the discrimination and systematic observation of self-statements, with self-monitoring of inappropriate behaviour.
3. Training in the fundamentals of problem solving, by which is meant defining the problem, anticipating the consequences and evaluating the feedback.
4. Modelling the self-statements associated with overt and cognitive skills.
5. Modelling and rehearsal of realistic self-evaluation and of coping skills.
6. The use of various procedures such as relaxation training, and coping imagery.
7. *In vivo* behavioural assignments.

Coping-skills packages can be complex and should be as comprehensive as possible, with a variety of techniques being taught to help meet the demands of the situations to be encountered.

Table 6.1 provides an example of one client's stress inoculation training chart which was used in therapy. This is a summary of his negative cognitions and statements used to deal with them, which enabled him successfully to reach the target.

Meichenbaum (1977) has provided some limited indications of the effectiveness of the technique, but has noted the

Table 6.1 Stress inoculation training chart

Event: visiting a crowded shop	
Negative thoughts	I cannot go in there, I will probably faint or be sick. If I go in I shall have to rush out and I will look foolish.
Preparation statements	(i) No problem – I have been getting on fine with my other targets – all I need to do is relax.
	(ii) If I can't stand it any more, I have a friend there who understands and we shall just leave.
Confrontation statements	(i) It's a large store but has lots of doors and the car is nearby when I want to leave.
	(ii) Most people will not even notice me – they are too busy shopping.
Coping statements	(i) Although I feel slightly peculiar and uncomfortable, I can cope in smaller shops – this really isn't very different.
	(ii) I have never fainted in a public place, so the chances are I won't here.

absence of many well-controlled trials. Barrios and Shigetomi (1979) concluded from their review of coping skills procedures that ' ... the research data support self-statement modification techniques as effective over no-treatment and attention placebo in reducing anxiety, as measured by self-report and behavioural techniques'. (Barrios and Shigetomi 1979, p.510) However, they also remarked that the data comparing self-statement modification with other types of treatments are mixed. For example, Holroyd (1976) demonstrated that the modification of self-statements was superior to desensitization, as did Goldfried, Lineham and Smith (1978), when the problem being treated was test anxiety. On the other hand, Emmelkamp, Kuipers and Eggeraat (1978) have shown that flooding is superior to self-statement modification in the treatment of agoraphobics. As yet, although a degree of optimism may be permissible, the status of self-statement modification with anxious subjects must remain equivocal. However, a number of evaluative studies are under way, and firm evidence should be available before long.

Combined therapeutic procedures

Recently there has been a trend towards treating the client with a combination of approaches – a 'therapeutic package' – and a concomitant decline in the number of reports of straightforward desensitization or flooding. The reason for this would seem to be twofold. The actual numbers of clients presenting with pure single phobias are extremely low. More common is a condition where the anxiety is generalized to a number of different situations or events, or is 'free-floating', i.e. apparently not related to any specific external event. The other reason behind combined-treatment development is the advent and increasing interest in cognitive methods. There is a school of thought that the behaviour-therapy methods of desensitization and flooding are simply not sophisticated enough to deal with complex interpersonal/interactional problems. Some form of direct behaviour change is frequently a part of these approaches, but it can be seen that talking and analysing verbal behaviour form a substantial part of cognitive treatment.

A typical example of a combined approach is illustrated by Stravynski (1984), who reports a case study in which a 45-year-old man with social deficits was helped to achieve greater social competence by a combination of treatment approaches. This man presented suffering from low mood and tension headaches. He had a long history of social difficulties, but this had been exacerbated after his wife left him. Certain target behaviours were ordered in a hierarchy relating to increasingly more challenging social situations, culminating in spending 30 minutes with a woman at lunch. The treatment 'package' consisted of the following ingredients: modelling, instructions or suggestions that may be useful for performance of the target behaviour; role rehearsal in a 'safe' situation with a surrogate; feedback on performance; self-monitoring of frequency of performance and level of anxiety experienced; cognitive modification of maladaptive thoughts; and homework assignments. Systematic data collection showed that a reduction of subjective anxiety and an increased frequency of target performance both resulted from the introduction of the treatment method.

There is currently a substantial move towards a mixed therapeutic approach in which more attention is given to what people say to themselves. However, it is also apparent that many of the cognitive therapies do continue to rely heavily on behavioural rehearsal as an element of the treatment approach. A combination of methods in the form of a therapeutic 'package' is becoming the norm rather than the exception, and this is particularly the case with clients who complain of a generalized anxiety state as opposed to those with single clear-cut phobias which in clinical practice are a considerably rarer phenomenon. Work undertaken by the authors in anxiety management classes, which will be more fully described in the next chapter, typifies what is becoming an increasing trend.

Although these combined treatment packages do allow the clinician a greater flexibility in drawing on a wider array of therapeutic tools, the importance of empirical validation must not take a back seat. The package of coping skills used by the authors in their group approach relies on methods that have already been supported individually by experimental findings. However, whatever the mode of delivery, it is important to demonstrate that combining methods in the treatment approach does have particular additional advantages. Combining treatment approaches could make them more complex and lengthier. Therefore, we need to know whether this is justified; there is no point in operating a complex therapeutic package if a simpler, more direct method could be just as effective.

Behavioural group therapy

The great majority of the studies described in the preceding sections have focused their attention on the modification of the various anxieties presented by individual clients. However, in recent years there has been an expansion of interest in conducting behavioural group therapy. Evidence for this can be taken from the establishment of an annual review series, *Behavioural group therapy*, first published only a few years ago (Upper and Ross 1979). It must be acknowledged that group therapy of a psychodynamic orientation has had a much longer tradition, but this has not usually had as its explicit target the modification of clients' behaviour.

An obvious argument for conducting therapy of any kind in groups is that it is much more economical of therapist time, and therefore money, than individual treatment. This economic argument is, indeed, a compelling one, but there are a number of additional advantages that can be gained from conducting behavioural interventions in groups. Harris (1977) points out that group members are able to provide an additional source of positive reinforcement for improved performance in behaviour, as well as that coming from the leader. Secondly, the group provides an opportunity for social modelling and observational learning which is less easily provided in individual treatment. Behavioural rehearsal and role-playing may be carried out more realistically in groups, since there is a broader base of individual styles to be tapped. A further advantage is that each group member has the opportunity to teach other participants; as clients learn treatment procedures, they may demonstrate them to the other members, leading to more peer group sharing of experiences. Eayrs (1981) has also pointed out that group approaches may allow the therapist to gain greater control over the consequences of a client's behaviour. This may be done by using group rules and contracts to make specific targets explicit. This stated public commitment may increase the chance of such targets being achieved; group approval or disapproval of a member's behaviour is a powerful contingency.

Behavioural group therapy might be taken initially to be a unified treatment method, but Flowers (1979) has distinguished three different meanings that it might have.

1. Behaviour therapy in groups

In its first meaning, it refers to the practice of a behavioural technique hitherto used with individuals, but now being used in a group setting. Lazarus (1961) may have been the first behaviour therapist to use a group in this way when he conducted a group desensitization procedure. In such groups it is usual for the client population to be a homogeneous one with similar problems, such as sharing the same specific phobia. The style of intervention is identical to that performed in individual treatment; client interaction is not considered important, and when it does occur, it is usually highly structured. However, although client interaction may not be encouraged, Lazarus (1961) commented that his group desensitization procedure was facilitated by the subjects being able to talk to each other. Katahn, Strenger and Cherry (1966) made a similar observation from their work in desensitizing college students with test anxiety. Flowers (1979) considers that although there are undoubtedly some differential effects when a behavioural intervention is carried out in a group rather than individually, these effects do not change the basic therapy.

Behaviour therapy in groups has most commonly been carried out on test-anxious college students and has, by and large, produced a good outcome. Suinn (1968), Crighton and Jehu (1969), Nawas, Fishman and Pucel (1970) and McManus (1971) have all conducted desensitization groups with generally favourable results. *In vivo* group exposure for agoraphobics has also been demonstrated to be an effective procedure (Hand, Lamontagne and Marks 1974), and Hafner and Marks (1976) have indicated that agoraphobics treated by group exposure did slightly better than those treated individually.

2. The use of behavioural principles in psychotherapeutic groups

The second meaning of behavioural group therapy has been the use of specific behavioural interventions within an existing psychotherapy group. In this case, the problems of individual group members may be extremely varied, and the style of the group may often be 'eclectic', which may be taken to mean that the therapist does whatever he or she feels will produce positive change (Flowers 1979).

Usually one behavioural intervention is employed, and the other interventions are not all specifically behavioural. Often, the behavioural intervention has been employed to increase verbal participation, perhaps by selectively re-inforcing each member's remarks with therapist attention (Rickard and Timmons 1961; Wagner 1966). Other targets mentioned by Flowers (1979) include conditioning against silence, conditioning on-task behaviour during the group sessions, the use of reinforcement to increase cohesion and the rewarding of self-disclosure.

3. Behavioural group therapy

The third meaning of behavioural group therapy is exemplified in a group where behavioural forms of inter-vention are performed in and by the group. This type of group is much more sophisticated than the earlier 'behaviour therapy in groups' described previously. Two main developments have characterized this new approach. The first of these has been the adoption of an educational model which emphasizes the teaching of behavioural principles rather than techniques. Clients are taught self-management skills which enable them to analyse and modify their own behaviour, thus enabling a variety of different problems to be dealt with in a single group. The advantage of this approach is that it allows more complex problems to be tackled in the group.

The second development which is important in defining behavioural group therapy is that the group itself is actively used as a medium for carrying out the treatment. The full advantages of using the group for peer and social modelling, behavioural rehearsal, role-playing and providing positive and negative feedback come strongly into play. Flowers (1979) comments that this type of group therapy is still emerging and does not fully exist at present. Nevertheless, some studies seem to be directed towards this style of therapy, e.g. Johnson (1975), Lawrence and Sundel (1972) and Rose (1977).

Despite the almost complete lack of published results on the efficacy of behavioural group therapy, there are a number of compelling reasons which commend its use. Not least of these reasons is the obvious economy which it allows in therapist time. Most busy clinicians should welcome any procedure which promises to reduce their waiting lists more effectively, and this reason alone may be responsible for a large part of the current interest being shown in group methods.

It is also notable that the most widely researched methods of treating anxiety are those which have had their greatest relevance in dealing with specific fears. Generalized anxiety is much more common than phobic states, yet the vast bulk of psychological research on anxiety has concerned itself with phobias. While the earlier attempts at behaviour therapy in groups also tended to concentrate on specific phobias, the emergence of behavioural group therapy has meant that more complex and varied problems can be accommodated in a single group. This suggests that a behavioural group might be a most appropriate medium for treating generalized anxiety problems.

The application of group methods is an area of great promise. The content of a group 'package' can be extremely flexible, incorporating a wide number of both behavioural and cognitive methods. The same caveat applies here, however, as applied to the use of combined treatment methods; it must not be assumed that the treatment will be more effective simply because it is more complex.

Chapter 7

The helping agencies

Where, then, do people with anxiety problems go to receive help? Firstly, it must be said that the majority of people who suffer the discomfort caused by intense or prolonged anxiety actually do not seek help anywhere, apart from their own resources and perhaps friends and relatives. This may be particularly the case if they are able to identify a specific cause or antecedent to the discomfort that they are experiencing. We all go through life and accept that there are ups and downs, and we do not run to the doctor each time we suffer some crisis. For example, maybe we have some important exam or a driving test to pass which is anxiety-provoking but short-lived and in the main not debilitating. Or, there are the crises related to interpersonal relationships which cause emotional upheaval from time to time but are accepted as part of 'life's rich tapestry' and recognized as being 'cured' best by the passage of time and with the support of close friends.

However, the passage of time does not always offer relief and sometimes only seems to serve to increase the anxiety symptoms. Or else there are occasions when there seems to be no recognizable cause, which leads to further worry and concern about one's health. There are a number of courses of action open to the anxious individual seeking help. These may roughly be divided into the self-help and the professional agencies.

Self-help agencies

There are a variety of agencies which aim to assist people
with emotional difficulties. Some, such as telephone-answer
services (e.g. the Samaritans or student Lifeline), offer a
general round-the-clock relief service. Many localities have
phobic societies, for example for people suffering from
agoraphobia. Individuals may refer themselves for help and
will be invited to join in meetings along with fellow-sufferers,
provided that they have found the appropriate agency for
their type of problem. The aim of such self-help groups is
generally to offer support and understanding from other
people who are able to closely identify with the problem
expressed. This sharing with fellow sufferers is seen as a
major strength of the self-help movement. It comes as a great
relief to many people who have felt isolated, misunderstood
or odd, and who may well have met with little sympathy
from other friends and relatives from whom they may have
sought help. The usefulness of sharing mutual problems
cannot be underestimated. However, these sorts of groups
are open to the criticism that they reinforce 'illness'; the mere
fact that the 'admission ticket' is having the problem and
getting better leads to the sometimes difficult prospect of
severance from this substantial support. Furthermore, it is
possible that in a 'deviant' group there may arise a value
system in which status is achieved by the greatest deviance,
i.e. the most severely debilitating problem. It is probably true
to say that there is a variable awareness of these dangers in
the self-help groups themselves and many seek to obviate
these dangers by organizing visiting speakers and some form
of input from the professional world. Others encourage
people by valuing progress towards 'normality' and re-
assuring them that links with the group need not be severed
until the individual is completely ready to do so. There has
been little in the way of objective evaluation of self-help
therapy groups, although anecdotal accounts suggest that
for some, at least, this form of help has been entirely
successful. When this is the case, self-help has the undoubted
advantage for the individual of avoiding the stigma

frequently attached to professional agencies such as psychiatric hospitals or the long-term and sometimes debilitating dependence on either drug therapy or psycho-therapy.

In addition to self-help in the form of societies or group therapies, there is an ever-growing library of books and pamphlets. These are aimed at people who have specific phobias, generalized problems with 'their nerves', or who would like to order their lives in more effective, rewarding ways. Judging by the growing number of books in this area, there is no doubt of the market. However, it is difficult to evaluate either their usefulness to the general public, or their efficacy as a mode of help. In a survey by Glasgow and Rosen (1978) it was concluded that the validation of available self-help behaviour therapy manuals was extremely variable at the time of writing. Further research was needed using clinically relevant subjects and assessment on the basis of clinical effectiveness as well as cost-effectiveness. As with the other forms of self-help, the 'do-it-yourself' manual has certain advantages. The main one is that it nurtures in the individual the satisfaction and self-esteem from coping independently with difficulties, and similarly avoids some of the problems associated with overdependence on outside agencies. However, as mentioned, effectiveness remains unknown and if the individual fails to improve, he or she may then sink into despair and finally present to the professional agencies with a fairly pessimistic attitude towards the chances of overcoming his or her problems.

There has recently been an increase in the use of combined self-help with professional guidance which utilizes self-help manuals with the back-up of professional home-visits, clinic appointments or telephone contact. This development will be discussed more fully in the next section.

The professional agencies

The involvement of professionals may either be the first port of call or, alternatively, the end point of a succession of failed attempts at self-help. Whichever it is, the starting point is usually a visit to the GP.

Drug treatments

Doctors have been shown to be differentially disposed to view their clients' problems at some point along an organic–functional continuum (Crombie 1963) and thereby will tend to diagnose and treat accordingly. Those with an 'organic bias' are likely to focus on the physical symptoms presented and look for physical causes, and may try a number of drug treatments and/or physiological investigations. In some cases the symptomatic relief may be all that is necessary. Others may be more predisposed to look for underlying emotional problems in the client's life. However, in spite of being aware of the functional nature of many of the presenting complaints or symptoms, the treatment may frequently (too frequently in the eyes of many) be the prescription of anxiolytic medication, which may lead to long-term dependency. The dangers of long-term treatment by the benzodiazepine group of drugs, such as Valium, Librium and Ativan, have been highlighted in a report by the Committee on the Review of Medicines (1980). The main findings of this review were related to efficacy and safety. It noted that there was little evidence that benzodiazepines are efficacious in the treatment of anxiety after four months. The Committee recommended that a warning regarding long-term efficacy should be given, 'particularly in view of the high proportion of patients receiving repeated prescriptions for extended periods of time'. It was also noted that although true addiction was rare, withdrawal symptoms, including anxiety, nausea, insomnia, tremor and apprehension, might occur on abrupt withdrawal of benzodiazepine therapy. The particular concern expressed was that these symptoms might suggest to the doctor that treatment had proved inadequate, and a further course might be prescribed, thus perpetuating the problem.

Although benzodiazepines are the most frequently chosen drugs for anxiety, there is some evidence for the effectiveness of other drugs. These include small doses of some major tranquillizers, but although these have the advantage that drug dependence does not develop, they are usually less preferred because of the risk of severe side-effects. Anti-depressants such as the monoamine oxidase inhibitors or tricyclics are sometimes prescribed when there is evidence of depression in addition to anxiety, and they are reported to have some anxiolytic effect as well as being antidepressant. Another group of drugs occasionally used in the treatment of anxiety states are the 'beta-blockers', which are used in low dosages. The specific advantages of the beta-blockers over other anxiolytic drugs are still being investigated, but there is some evidence that they may have a more specific effect on certain physical symptoms, and less of a sedative effect (Tyrer and Lader 1974).

Referral to a psychologist

The frequency with which GPs refer patients to a psychiatric colleague is variable and is related to such factors as length of outpatient waiting list, geographical location, professional or personal acquaintance, and even the degree of confidence felt by the GP in dealing with neurotic problems. The normal course of action would be to refer to a hospital-based psychiatrist, although this may vary in different parts of the country according to the facilities locally available. There is an increasing tendency for GPs to refer direct to a clinical psychologist or in some cases to a community psychiatric nurse. Psychiatrists, psychologists and community psychiatric nurses may also spend sessions attached to general practices, and this makes referral to them much more straightforward. When these specialists have a base in general practice, it encourages two-way communication between them and the GPs. It also removes some of the obstacles felt by people referred to outpatient clinics based in psychiatric hospitals; there is still a tendency for people to see these as places for 'mad people', and there is often a sense of stigma felt by those attending.

The main subject matter of this book has been on

psychological therapies, predominantly those springing from the behaviourist tradition, and it is on these that we will focus. When a client is referred for treatment to a psychiatrist or psychologist, there will be a period of assessment during which it will be decided which is likely to be the best form of help. For example, if the individual is primarily suffering from tension and finding it difficult to relax, or sleep, then he or she may be advised on relaxation methods. These may be taught in the clinic, either by direct instruction from a psychologist or possibly another professional such as an occupational therapist or physiotherapist. In some cases, tape-recorded instructions may be used, and these can be taken home for use there. The individual must also be instructed in ways of applying the skill in the normal routine of everyday life. If the problems are more complex, for example involving specific phobias or a generalized anxiety state related to environmental causes, the client will be seen over a prolonged period of weeks or months and counselled in one or more of the techniques described in Chapters 5 and 6.

These forms of treatment will ordinarily be conducted on an outpatient basis, admission to hospital being considered in only a minority of circumstances. This may be necessary for a number of reasons, such as the need for physical investigations to be conducted, to allow monitoring if drugs are to be used, or if the contingencies in the home situation are such that the individual requires a respite to gain control and learn alternative coping strategies away from the continued presence of the initial causes of anxiety.

However, removing the person from the natural environment can create its own problems for the therapist, relating to the generalization of new skills back into the old environment. It is one thing to learn to be relaxed and to cope with life in the sheltered environment of a hospital with plenty of support, and another thing altogether to maintain these changes when faced with the outside world again. For this reason it is important to maintain support at an outpatient level once the client has been discharged.

More recently, there has been a move to explore ways of improving outpatient help by the therapist going into the individual's home situation and observing the client in the natural environment – designing a therapist-guided self-help programme. For example, Matthews *et al.* (1977) have reported on a home-based treatment programme for agoraphobic people which utilizes the individual's existing support systems such as neighbourhood contacts and spouses. Contact is made on a regular basis by home visits and telephone calls, while the client has specific assignments to do and reports back on progress. This approach is usually supplemented with a written manual of instruction for the client to follow in so far as the pace can be self-directed, and the onus is on the client to meet the mutually agreed behavioural targets. In this way a number of the dependency, stigmatization and generalization problems can be avoided. In addition, this method has the advantage over independent self-help, because the client does have access to professional help, when required.

Treatment in groups

As mentioned in the previous chapter, there has been a move towards the running of coping-skills groups for anxiety sufferers. A strong argument for conducting therapy in groups is that it is much more economical of therapist time and therefore money than individual treatment. This is not the only argument that can be made in favour of group treatments, and a number of other advantages were indicated at the end of Chapter 6.

Behavioural groups for anxiety management have become increasingly popular in recent years. The authors have conducted a research programme in which we evaluated the effectiveness of such groups. We have also run the groups in a variety of settings including hospital outpatient clinics, university clinics, general practices and, more recently, in an Adult Education Centre as an evening class (Eayrs, Rowan and Harvey 1984; Rowan and Eayrs in press). The treatment model adopted in these groups was one which viewed therapy as an educational training. This view of therapy as education was preferred to the traditional 'medical' model since it emphasizes self-management strategies, encouraging clients to analyse and change their own behaviour. They became active participants in setting their own targets, developing new skills and carrying out 'homework' tasks in naturalistic settings.

The coping-skills course ran over a period of ten weeks during which time there were eight scheduled meetings. The first six meetings were held weekly and the final two fortnightly. This was to allow time for completion of homework tasks and the practice of new skills in the home situation. Each meeting lasted $1\frac{1}{2}$ hours and followed a broadly similar format. Firstly, the groups discussed their homework assignments and any problems that might have arisen. Therapists gave feedback and help as necessary. The next part of the meeting was the introduction of a new coping skill, its demonstration and rehearsal, or else revision of previously learned ones. At some point roughly half-way through the meeting there would be a coffee break, during which time the therapists left the group on its own. The final part of the meeting was taken up by further discussion of the new skill, its application in individual circumstances and any anticipated difficulties. Specific homework tasks were set and written handouts and self-monitoring sheets given out.

The course comprised a series of coping skills which were taken from the current clinical literature on anxiety management. These included muscle relaxation using a modified Jacobsonian (progressive tensing–relaxing) method; mental relaxation which was a procedure based on the method of anxiety management training developed by Suinn and Richardson (1971); target setting; self-reinforcement; positive self-talk derived from self-instructional training of Meichenbaum (1974). Written handouts were prepared on each of the course elements and given out as each skill was covered. The group members were also instructed in simple self-monitoring procedures such as self-rating of subjective tension level before and after relaxation. A rigid timetable was avoided, so although each group completed the course, the order of presentation and emphasis placed on each component varied according to the demands of each group.

After having run many groups in health settings, either hospitals or health centres, it became clear that they were effective and worth while. However, since the classes were run on educational lines, there was the possibility that they might be even more successful if moved from a health-care setting to an educational one. It was felt that the client group which would be attracted to such a class would be more amenable to working within the educational model which the authors were keen to exploit. It had become apparent that most of the clients seen in the hospital found it very difficult to stop being 'patients' and to take an active part in their own 'treatment'. Most previous clients who had attended the hospital classes were still expecting to have something done to them to 'cure' them, and a good deal of effort was expended in trying to reorient them. However, it was reasoned that people attending an educational establishment would be much more willing to be taught procedures which they could apply to their own problems.

It was also hoped that those clients attending might have problems of shorter duration than those seen in the hospital setting since there is some evidence to suggest that the less chronically incapacitated clients make better progress. It is, unfortunately, an all too common occurrence that hospital-based psychology departments are at the end of a long referral chain, and the clients who are eventually referred often have a long history of unsatisfactory or unsuccessful treatment. If clients had the opportunity to refer themselves directly for help, it was hoped that they would be seen before their problems had had time to develop.

It was for this reason that it was considered desirable to establish an anxiety management group as part of the evening-class curriculum in a local education centre. This fulfilled the aim of encouraging an educational perspective and it had the added advantage that the clients were completely self-referred.

When the local education department was contacted they were extremely willing to include a course in anxiety management as part of their syllabus. In the first year of this course, 19 people registered for the term. In general, the results of the course gave encouragement to the notion that anxiety management techniques can be taught effectively outside a health setting and that an evening class such as this is a viable project.

As a general rule, those attending the evening class were experiencing anxiety symptoms which were just as severe as those experienced by the people attending hospital groups. It is also of some interest that more than half the regular attenders were being seen by a 'specialist', i.e. someone other than a GP, for the first time. In other words, the evening class seemed to be reaching a number of individuals who may not have sought help by following the more usual channels.

It is hard to say whether the acceptance of an educational model was made easier by running the class in an educational setting. We have no hard evidence to offer on this issue, but we formed some impressions. These impressions are based on the comments made by the class members themselves, and these suggested that the educational model was being accepted. For example, one lady commented on her course evaluation form:

> During the first few weeks I somehow got the impression that the class folded its arms, sat back and said 'OK, teach me how to cope with my anxiety' as though there were glib textbook solutions. But as the class went on they began to participate more and more and started to work out ways of tackling their problems.

While firm conclusions are difficult to draw from this new approach to teaching anxiety management skills, there has been a wide interest shown in the idea of offering such a course as part of the evening-class syllabus. It has been the subject of a radio programme and interest has been expressed by a number of different education authorities in mounting similar classes.

Conducting a class in an adult education centre is undoubtedly a departure from offering anxiety management in a hospital or other health centre, but other ventures might allow greater access to the methods. For example, it might be possible to give regular broadcasts of an anxiety management course on radio or television, thus opening up access to a great many potential clients. Since the evening-class study demonstrated that the methods could be taught with some success to a self-selected audience, the suggestion of, say, televised courses seems quite feasible.

Conclusions

It can be seen then that several new trends in the treatment of clinical anxiety are emerging. It has become increasingly clear that most anxiety problems evolve and are maintained by a complex set of circumstances in an individual's life and that these need to be understood more thoroughly if a treatment is to be of lasting benefit. There has therefore, been a move away from simple prescriptions of either drugs or behaviour therapy techniques towards teaching the client a greater understanding of the determinants of the problem and a combination of skills or self-management methods to deal with it, increasingly in the form of combined treatment packages. While the recognition of the need to develop more sophisticated treatment approaches is laudable, it does present a greater challenge for evaluation. There is still a considerable need to test properly the various treatment packages to continue the tradition of the original, simpler behaviour therapies in establishing firm empirical foundations for clinical use.

References

Agras, S., Sylvester, D. and Oliveau, D. (1969) The epidemiology of common fears and phobias, *Comparative Psychiatry,* **10**, 151–6.

Bandura, A. (1969) *Principles of Behaviour Modification.* New York: Rinehart and Winston.

Bandura, A. (1971) Psychotherapy based upon modelling principles. In A. E. Bergin and S. L. Garfield (Eds), *Handbook of Psychotherapy and Behaviour change: an empirical analysis.* New York: Wiley.

Bandura, A., Blanchard, E. B. and Ritter, B. (1969) The relative efficacy of desensitization and modelling approaches for inducing behavioural, affective and attitudinal changes, *Journal of Personality and Social Psychology,* **13**, 173–99.

Bandura, A., Grusec, J. E. and Menlove, F. L. (1967) Vicarious extinction of avoidance behaviour, *Journal of Personality and Social Psychology,* **5**, 16–23.

Bandura, A., Jeffery, R. W. and Gajdos, E. (1975) Generalizing change through self-directed performance, *Behaviour Research and Therapy,* **13**, 141–52.

Bandura, A., Jeffery, R. W. and Wright, C. L. (1974) Efficacy of participant modelling as a function of response induction aids, *Journal of Abnormal Psychology,* **83**, 56–64.

Bandura, A. and Menlove, F. I. (1968) Factors determining vicarious extinction of avoidance behaviour through symbolic modelling, *Journal of Personality and Social Psychology,* **8**, 99–108.

Barrios, B. A. and Shigetomi, C. C. (1979) Coping skills training for the management of anxiety: A critical review, *Behaviour Therapy*, **10**, 491–522.

Beck, A. T. (1976) *Cognitive Therapy and Emotional Disorders*. New York: International Universities Press.

Beck, A. T. and Rush, A. J. (1975) A cognitive model of anxiety formation and anxiety resolution. In I. G. Sarason and C. D. Spielberger (Eds), *Stress and Anxiety*, Vol. 2. New York: Wiley.

Benson, H. (1975) *The Relaxation Response*. London: Collins.

Bernstein, D. A. and Paul, G. L. (1971) Some comments on therapy analogue research with small animal 'phobias', *Journal of Behaviour Therapy and Experimental Psychiatry*, **2**, 225–39.

Blackburn, I. M., Bishop, S., Glen, A. I. M., Whalley, L. J. and Christie, L. E. (1981) The efficacy of cognitive therapy in depression: A treatment trial using cognitive therapy and pharmacotherapy, each alone and in combination, *British Journal of Psychiatry*, **39**, 181–9.

Blanchard, E. B. (1970) The relative contributions of modelling, informational influences, and physical contact in the extinction of phobic behaviour, *Journal of Abnormal Psychology*, **76**, 55–61.

Borkovec, T. D. (1973) The effects of instructional suggestion and physiological cues on analogue fear, *Behaviour Therapy*, **4**, 185–92.

Borkovec, T. D. and Rachman, S. (1979) The utility of analogue research, *Behaviour Research and Therapy*, **17**, 253–61.

Borkovec, T. D., Weerts, T. C. and Bernstein, D. A. (1977) Assessment of anxiety. In A. R. Ciminero, K. S. Calhoun and H. E. Adams (Eds), *Handbook of Behavioural Assessment*. New York: Wiley.

Braun, P. R. and Reynolds, D. N. (1969) A factor analysis of a 100-item fear survey inventory, *Behaviour Research and Therapy*, **7**, 399–402.

Bregman, E. O. (1934) An attempt to modify the emotional attitudes of infants by the conditioned response technique, *Journal of Genetic Psychology*, **45**, 169–98.

Carr, A. T. (1979) The psychopathology of fear. In W. Sluckin (Ed.), *Fear in Animals and Man*. New York: Van Nostrand Reinhold.

Carroll, D. (1984) *Biofeedback in Practice*. Harlow: Longman.

Committee on the Review of Medicines (1980) Systematic review of the benzodiazepines, *British Medical Journal*, 29 March.

Coué, E. (1922) *The Practice of Autosuggestion*. New York: Doubleday.

Crighton, J. and Jehu, D. (1969) Treatment of examination anxiety by systematic desensitization or psychotherapy in groups, *Behaviour Research and Therapy*, 7, 245–8.

Crombie, D. L. (1963) The Procrustean bed of medical nomenclature, *The Lancet*, June 1, 1205–6.

Davison, G. C. and Wilson, G. T. (1973) Processes of fear-reduction in systematic desensitization: Cognitive and social reinforcement factors in humans, *Behaviour Therapy*, 4, 1–21.

Di Loreto, A. O. (1971) *Comparative Psychotherapy: an experimental analysis*. Chicago: Aldine-Atherton.

Eayrs, C. B. (1981) *Behavioural group therapy: Teaching coping skills for anxiety management*. Unpublished doctoral dissertation, University of Birmingham.

Eayrs, C. B., Rowan, D. C. and Harvey, P. G. (1984) Behavioural group training for anxiety management, *Behavioural Psychotherapy*, 12, 117–29.

Ellis, A. (1962) *Reason and Emotion in Psychotherapy*. New York: Stuart.

Ellis, A. (1970) *The Essence of Rational Psychotherapy: a comprehensive approach to treatment*. New York: Institute for Rational Living.

Ellis, A. (1971) *Growth Through Reason*. Palo Alto, California: Science and Behaviour Books.

Emmelkamp, P. M. G., Kuipers, A. C. M. and Eggeraat, J. B. (1978) Cognitive modification versus prolonged exposure *in vivo*: A comparison with agoraphobics as subjects, *Behaviour Research and Therapy*, 16, 33–41.

English, H. B. (1929) Three cases of the 'conditioned fear response', *Journal of Abnormal and Social Psychology*, 34, 221–5.

Eysenck, H. J. (1968) A theory of the incubation of anxiety/fear responses, *Behaviour Research and Therapy*, 6, 309–21.

Eysenck, H. J. (1976) The learning theory model of neurosis: A new approach, *Behaviour Research and Therapy*, 14, 251–67.

Eysenck, H. J. (1980) Psychological theories of anxiety. In G. D. Burrows and B. Davies (Eds), *Handbook of Studies on Anxiety*. Amsterdam: Elsevier/North-Holland Biomedical Press.

Flowers, J. V. (1979) Behavioural analysis of group therapy and a model for behavioural group therapy. In D. Upper and S. M. Ross (Eds), *Behavioural Group Therapy, 1979: an annual review*. Champaign, Illinois: Research Press Company.

Garcia, J. and Koelling, R. A. (1966) Relation of cue to consequence in avoidance learning, *Psychonomic Science*, 4, 123–4.

Geer, J. H. (1965) The development of a scale to measure fear, *Behaviour Research and Therapy*, 3, 45–53.

Gelder, M. G., Bancroft, J. H. J., Garth, D. H., Johnston, D. W., Matthews, A. M. and Shaw, P. M. (1973) Specific and non-specific factors in behaviour therapy, *British Journal of Psychiatry*, 123, 445–62.

Glasgow, R. E. and Rosen, G. M. (1978) Behavioural bibliotherapy: A review of self-help behaviour therapy manuals, *Psychological Bulletin*, 85, 1–23.

Goldberg, D. P. (1972) *The detection of psychiatric illness by questionnaire*. Maudsley Monograph Number 22, London: Oxford University Press.

Goldfried, M. R. (1971) Systematic desensitization as training in self-control, *Journal of Consulting and Clinical Psychology*, 37, 228–34.

Goldfried, M. R., Decenteceo, E. T. and Weinberg, L. (1974) Systematic rational restructuring as a self-control technique, *Behaviour Therapy*, 5, 247–54.

Goldfried, M. R., Lineham, M. M. and Smith, J. L. (1978) Reduction of text anxiety through cognitive restructuring, *Journal of Consulting and Clinical Psychology*, 46, 32–9.

Goodman, D. S. and Maultsby, M. C. (1974) *Emotional Well-being Through Rational Behaviour Training*. Springfield, Illinois: Thomas.

Hafner, J. and Marks, I. M. (1976) Exposure in vivo of agoraphobics: Contributions of diazepam, group exposure and anxiety evocation, *Psychological Medicine*, 6, 71–88.

Hallam, R. S. and Rachman, S. (1976) Current status of aversion therapy. In M. Hersen, R. Eisler and P. Miller (Eds), *Progress in Behavioural Modification*, Vol. II. New York: Academic Press.

Hand, I., Lamontagne, Y. and Marks, I. M. (1974) Group exposure (flooding) in vivo for agoraphobics, *British Journal of Psychiatry*, 124, 588–602.

Harris, G. G. (Ed.) (1977) The Group Treatment of Human

Problems: a social learning approach. New York: Grune and Stratton.

Herzberg, A. (1941) Short treatment of neuroses by graduated tasks, *British Journal of Medical Psychology*, **19**, 19–36.

Hodgson, R. and Rachman, S. (1974) Desynchrony in measures of fear, *Behaviour Research and Therapy*, **12**, 319–26.

Holroyd, K. A. (1976) Cognition and desensitization in the group treatment of test anxiety, *Journal of Consulting and Clinical Psychology*, **44**, 991–1001.

Hugdahl, K. (1981) The three-systems-model of fear and emotion – a critical examination, *Behaviour Research and Therapy*, **19**, 75–85.

Jacobson, E. (1938) *Progressive Relaxation*. Chicago: University of Chicago Press.

Janis, I. L. (1951) *Air War and Emotional Stress*. New York: McGraw-Hill.

Johnson, W. G. (1975) Group therapy: A behavioural perspective, *Behaviour Therapy*, **6**, 30–8.

Jones, M. C. (1924) The elimination of children's fears, *Journal of Experimental Psychology*, **7**, 383–90.

Katahn, M., Strenger, S. and Cherry, N. (1966) Group counselling and behaviour therapy with test-anxious college students, *Journal of Consulting Psychology*, **30**, 544–9.

Kazdin, A. E. and Wilcoxon, L. A. (1976) Systematic desensitization and nonspecific treatment effects: A methodological evaluation. *Psychological Bulletin*, **83**, 729–58.

Krapf, J. E. and Nawas, M. M. (1970) Differential ordering of stimulus presentation in systematic desensitization. *Journal of Abnormal Psychology*, **75**, 333–7.

Lacey, J. I. (1967) Somatic response patterning and stress: Some revisions of activation theory. In M. H. Appleby and R. R. Trumball (Eds), *Psychological Stress: issues in research*. New York: Appleton Century Crofts.

Lader, M. H. and Wing, L. (1966) *Physiological Measures, Sedative Drugs and Morbid Anxiety*. London: Oxford University Press.

Lang, P. J. (1970) Stimulus control, response control and desensitization. In D. Lewis (Ed.), *Learning Approaches to Therapeutic Behaviour*. Chicago: Aldine Press.

Lang, P. J. and Lazovik, A. D. (1963) Experimental desensitization of a phobia, *Journal of Abnormal and Social Psychology*, **66**, 519–25.

Lang, P. J., Melamed, B. G. and Hart, J. (1970) A psycho-physiological analysis of fear modification using an automated desensitization procedure, *Journal of Abnormal Psychology*, **76**, 220–34.

Lawrence, H. and Sundel, M. (1972) Behaviour modification in adult groups, *Social Work*, **17**, 34–43.

Lazarus, A. A. (1961) Group therapy of phobic disorders by systematic desensitization, *Journal of Abnormal and Social Psychology*, **63**, 505–10.

Lazarus, A. A. (1971) *Behaviour Therapy and Beyond*. New York: McGraw-Hill.

Lazarus, A. A. and Wilson, G. T. (1976) Behaviour modification: Clinical and experimental perspectives. In B. B. Wolman (Ed.), *The Therapist's Handbook: Treatment methods of mental disorders*. New York: Van Nostrand Reinhold.

Lazarus, R. S., Averill, J. R. and Opton, E. M. (1970) Toward a cognitive theory of emotion. In M. B. Arnold (Ed.), *Feelings and Emotion*. New York: Academic Press.

Levy, R. and Meyer, V. (1971) Ritual prevention in obsessional patients, *Proceedings of the Royal Society of Medicine*, **64**, 1115–18.

Lewis, A. (1942) Incidence of neurosis in England under war conditions, *Lancet*, **2**, 175–83.

Lick, J. R. and Katkin, E. S. (1976) Assessment of anxiety and fear. In M. Hersen and A. S. Bellack (Eds), *Behavioural Assessment: a practical handbook*. Oxford: Pergamon.

Luria, A. (1961) *The Role of Speech in the Regulation of Normal and Abnormal Behaviour*. New York: Liveright.

McManus, M. (1971) Group desensitization of test anxiety, *Behaviour Research and Therapy*, **9**, 51–6.

Mahoney, M. J. (1974) *Cognition and Behaviour Modification*. Cambridge: Ballinger.

Mahoney, M. J. and Arnkoff, D. B. (1978) Cognitive and self-control therapies. In S. L. Bergin and A. E. Garfield (Eds), *Handbook of Psychotherapy and Behaviour Change* (2nd edn). New York: Wiley.

Mandler, G. (1975) *Mind and Emotion*. New York: Wiley.

Marks, I. M. (1975) Behavioural treatments of phobic and obsessive-compulsive disorders: A critical appraisal. In M.

Hersen, R. M. Eisler and P. M. Miller (Eds), *Progress in Behaviour Modification*, Vol. 1. New York: Academic Press.

Marks, I. M. (1978a) *Living with Fear*. New York: McGraw-Hill.

Marks, I. M. (1978b) Behavioural psychotherapy of adult neurosis. In S. L. Bergin and A. E. Garfield (Eds), *Handbook of Psychotherapy and Behaviour Change* (2nd edn). New York: Wiley.

Marks, I. M., Boulougouris, J. C. and Marset, P. (1971) Flooding versus desensitization in the treatment of phobic patients: A crossover study, *British Journal of Psychiatry*, 119, 353–75.

Marks, I. M., Hodgson, R. and Rachman, S. (1975) Treatment of chronic obsessive-compulsive neurosis by *in vivo* exposure: A two-year follow-up and issues in treatment. *British Journal of Psychiatry*, 127, 349–64.

Marshall, W. L. (1981) Behavioural treatment of phobic and obsessive-compulsive disorders. In L. Michelson, M. Hersen and S. M. Turner (Eds), *Future Perspectives in Behaviour Therapy*. New York: Plenum.

Marshall, W. L., Gauthier, J. and Gordon, A. (1979) The current status of flooding therapy. In M. Hersen, R. M. Eisler and P. M. Miller (Eds), *Progress in Behaviour Modification, Vol. 7. New York: Academic Press.*

Matthews, A. M., Teasdale, J. D., Munby, M., Johnson, D. W. and Shaw, P. M. (1977) A home-based treatment programme for agoraphobia, *Behaviour Therapy*, 8, 915–24.

Meichenbaum, D. (1974) Self instructional methods. In F. H. Kaufer and A. P. Goldstein (Eds), *Helping People Change*. New York: Pergamon.

Meichenbaum, D. (1977) *Cognitive-behaviour Modification: an integrative approach*. New York: Plenum.

Meichenbaum, D. and Cameron, R. (1974) The clinical potential of modifying what clients say to themselves. In M. J. Majoney and C. E. Thoresen (Eds), *Self-control: power to the person*. Monterey: Brooks/Cole.

Miller, N. E. (1948) Studies of fear as an acquirable drive: 1. Fear as motivation and fear-reduction as reinforcement in the learning of new responses, *Journal of Experimental Psychology*, 38, 89–101.

Morganstern, K. P. (1973) Implosive therapy and flooding procedures: A critical review, *Psychological Bulletin*, 79, 318–34.

Mowrer, O. H. (1939) A stimulus-response analysis of anxiety and its role as a reinforcing agent, *Psychological Review*, 46, 553–65.

Mowrer, O. H. (1940) Anxiety-reduction and learning, *Journal of*

Experimental Psychology, **27**, 497–516.

Mowrer, O. H. (1960) *Learning Theory and the Symbolic Processes.* New York: Wiley.

Murray, E. J. and Foote, F. (1979) The origins of fears of snakes, *Behaviour Research and Therapy,* **17**, 489–95.

Napalkov, S. V. (1963) Information process and the brain. In N. Wiener and J. C. Schade (Eds), *Progress in Brain Research,* Vol. 2. Amsterdam: Elsevier.

Nawas, M., Fishman, S. and Pucel, J. (1970) A standardised desensitization programme applicable to group and individual treatments, *Behaviour Research and Therapy,* **8**, 49–56.

Nisbett, R. E. and Schachter, S. (1966) The cognitive manipulation of pain, *Journal of Experimental Social Psychology*, 227–36.

Ost, L-G and Hugdahl, K. (1981) Acquisition of phobias and anxiety response patterns in clinical patients. *Behaviour Research and Therapy,* **19**, 439–47.

Paul, G. L. (1966) *Insight v. Desensitization in Psychotherapy: an experiment in anxiety reduction.* Stanford: Stanford University Press.

Paul, G. L. (1969) Outcome of systematic desensitization II: Controlled investigations of individual treatment, technique variations and current status. In C. M. Franks (Ed.), *Behaviour Therapy: appraisal and status.* New York: McGraw-Hill.

Pavlov, I. P. (1927) *Conditioned Reflexes.* London: Oxford University Press.

Rachman, S. (1977) The conditioning theory of fear-acquisition: A critical examination, *Behaviour Research and Therapy,* **15**, 375–87.

Rachman, S. (1978a) Human fears: A three systems analysis, *Scandinavian Journal of Behaviour Therapy,* **7**, 237–45.

Rachman, S. (1978b) *Fear and Courage.* San Francisco: Freeman.

Rachman, S. and Hodgson, R. (1974) Synchrony and desynchrony in fear and avoidance, *Behaviour Research and Therapy,* **12**, 311–18.

Rachman, S., Hodgson, R. and Marks, I. M. (1971) The treatment of chronic obsessive-compulsive neurosis, *Behaviour Research and Therapy,* **9**, 237–48.

Rachman, S., Marks, I. M. and Hodgson, R. (1973) The treatment of obsessive-compulsive neurotics by modelling and flooding *in vivo*, *Behaviour Research and Therapy*, **11**, 463–71.

Rescorla, R. A. and Solomon, R. L. (1967) Two-process learning theory: Relationships between Pavlovian conditioning and instrumental learning, *Psychological Review*, **74**, 151–82.

Rickard, H. C. and Timmons, E. O. (1961) Manipulating verbal behaviour in groups: A comparison of three intervention techniques, *Psychological Reports*, **9**, 729–36.

Rimm, D. C., Janda, L. H., Lancaster, D. W., Nahl, M. and Dittmar, K. (1977) An exploratory investigation of the origin and maintenance of phobias, *Behaviour Research and Therapy.*, **15**, 231–8.

Rimm, D. C. and Masters, J. C. (1979) *Behaviour Therapy: techniques and empirical findings* (2nd edn). New York: Academic Press.

Ritter, B. (1968) The group desensitization of children's snake phobias using vicarious and contact desensitization procedures, *Behaviour Research and Therapy*, **6**, 1–6.

Rose, S. D. (1977) *Group Therapy: a behavioural approach*. Englewood Cliffs, New Jersey: Prentice-Hall.

Rosenman, R. H., Brand, R. J., Jenkins, C. D., Friedman, M., Strauss, R. and Wurm, M. (1975) Coronary heart disease in the Western Collaborative Group Study: Final follow-up experience of $8\frac{1}{2}$ years, *Journal of the American Medical Association*, **233**, 872–7.

Rowan, D. C. and Eayrs, C. B. (in press) Coping with anxiety: An adult education evening class, *Behavioural Psychotherapy*.

Royal College of General Practitioners (1974) *Morbidity Statistics from General Practice. Second National Study 1970–71*. The Office of Population Consensuses and Surveys, DHSS. London: HMSO.

Rush, A. J. and Watkins, J. T. (1981) Group versus individual cognitive therapy: A pilot study, *Cognitive Therapy and Research*, **5**, 95–103.

Schachter, S. (1971) *Emotion, Obesity and Crime*. New York: Academic Press.

Schachter, S. and Singer, J. E. (1962) Cognitive, social and physiological determinants of emotional state, *Psychological Review*, **69**, 379–99.

Schachter, S. and Wheeler, L. (1962) Epinephrine, chlorpromazine and amusement. *Journal of Abnormal and Social Psychology*, **65**,

121–8.

Schultz, J. H. and Luthe, W. (1959) *Autogenic Training*. New York: Grune and Stratton.

Seligman, M. E. P. (1970) On the generality of the laws of learning, *Psychological Review*, 77, 406–18.

Seligman, M. E. P. (1971) Phobias and preparedness, *Behaviour Therapy*, 2, 307–20.

Seligman, M. E. P. and Hager, J. (Eds) (1972) *Biological Boundaries of Learning*. New York: Appleton Century Crofts.

Seligman, M. E. P. and Johnston, J. C. (1973) A cognitive theory of avoidance learning. In F. J. McGuigan and D. B. Lumsden (Eds), *Contemporary Approaches to Conditioning and Learning*. Washington, D.C.: Winston.

Shepherd, M., Cooper, B., Brown, A. C. and Kalton, G. (1966) *Psychiatric Illness in General Practice*. London: Oxford University Press.

Sherman, A. R. (1972) Real-life exposure as a primary therapeutic factor in the desensitization treatment of fear, *Journal of Abnormal Psychology*, 79, 19–28.

Sims, A. C. P. (1983) *Neurosis in Society*. London: Macmillan.

Spielberger, C., Gorsuch, R. and Lushene, R. (1970) *Manual for the State-Trait Anxiety Inventory*. Palo Alto, California: Consulting Psychologist Press.

Stravynski, A. (1984) The use of broad conversational targets in social skills training to promote generalization of gains to real life: A case study, *Behavioural Psychotherapy*, 12, 61–7.

Sue, D. (1972) The role of relaxation in systematic desensitization, *Behaviour Research and Therapy*, 10, 157–8.

Suinn, R. M. (1968) The desensitization of test-anxiety by group and individual treatment, *Behaviour Research and Therapy*, 6, 385–7.

Suinn, R. M. (1969) The STABS, a measure of test anxiety for behaviour therapy: Normative data, *Behaviour Research and Therapy*, 7, 335–9.

Suinn, R. M. and Bloom, L. J. (1978) Anxiety management training for pattern A behaviour, *Journal of Behavioural Medicine*, 1, 25–35.

Suinn, R. M. and Richardson, F. (1971) Anxiety management training: A non-specific behaviour therapy program for anxiety control, *Behaviour Therapy*, 2, 498–510.

Taylor, J. A. (1953) A personality scale of manifest anxiety, *Journal of Abnormal and Social Psychology*, 48, 285–95.

Tyrer, P. and Lader, M. H. (1974) Response to propranolol and diazepam in somatic and psychic anxiety, *British Medical Journal*, ii, 14–16.

Upper, D. and Ross, S. M. (Eds) (1979) *Behavioural Group Therapy, 1979: an annual review.* Champaign, Illinois: Research Press Company.

Vygotsky, L. S. (1962) *Thought and Language.* Cambridge, Mass.: MIT Press.

Wagner, M. (1966) Reinforcement of verbal productivity in group therapy, *Psychological Reports,* **19**, 1217–18.

Walk, R. D. (1956) Self-ratings of fear in a fear-invoking situation, *Journal of Abnormal and Social Psychology,* **52**, 171–8.

Watson, J. B, and Rayner, R. (1920) Conditional and emotional reactions, *Journal of Experimental Psychology,* **3**, 1–14.

Watts, F. N., Powell, G. E. and Austin, S. V. (1973) The modification of abnormal beliefs, *British Journal of Medical Psychology,* **46**, 359–63.

Wilson, G. T. and Davison, G. C. (1971) Processes of fear reduction in systematic desensitization: Animal studies, *Psychological Bulletin,* **76**, 1–14.

Wolpe, J. (1954) Reciprocal inhibition as the main basis of psychotherapeutic effects, *Archives of Neurology and Psychiatry,* **72**, 205–26.

Wolpe, J. (1958) *Psychotherapy by Reciprocal Inhibition.* Stanford: Stanford University Press.

Wolpe, J. (1969) *The Practice of Behaviour Therapy.* New York: Pergamon.

Wolpe, J. and Lang, P. J. (1964) A fear survey schedule for use in behaviour therapy, *Behaviour Research and Therapy,* **2**, 27–30.

Wolpe, J. and Lazarus, A. A. (1966) *Behaviour Therapy Techniques.* New York: Pergamon.

Yates, A. J. (1975) *Theory and Practice in Behaviour Therapy.* New York: Wiley.

Zuckerman, M. (1960) The development of an effective adjective checklist for the measurement of anxiety. *Journal of Consulting Psychology,* **24**, 457–62.

Index